THE PRIEST

AWAKENING THE MODERN WOMAN

ASHA RAMAKRISHNA

The Priestess Code: Awakening the Modern Woman

The Priestess Code™ Series – Volume One

Asha Ramakrishna Guzman & Asha Ramakrishna Co., LLC

Harvard, MA. 01451

For requests to the publisher contact: asha@ashaisnow.com

Cover photo: Cyrissa Carlson

About Author photo: Julie Hesketh

Printed in the United States of America

First Printing, 2017

ISBN 978-0-9987647-0-2 eBook 978-0-9987647-1-9

Visit the author's website at ashaisnow.com

Dedication

I place The Priestess Code at the feet of the most Divine. My Beloved, my friend, my confidant. I would not know Her essence had it not been for *Carmencita*, my Beloved *abuela*. I dedicate this book to her and *La Virgen Del Valle* who both show me the power of being a woman devoted to Self, the world, and to the All that is.

Gratitude

ratitude to all those who have crossed my path as I wrote for nine years; those who inspired me with your stories and your wisdom.

A special gratitude to some of the teachers who have come before me: Paramahansa Yogananda, Burt Goldman, Lidia Scher, James Twyman, and John Wyrick. Thank you to the Sisters that support my spiritual wellbeing and expansion: Erica Rock and Christina Sophia Stellarum. Sweet thank you to two women who always make my life just a little easier: Jess McClear and Chris Morrison, you have both shown me true Sisterhood.

Gratitude to those who believed in this project and the quiet and sometimes roaring wisdom I bring. Karen Curry Parker you have been a midwife to this book from its infancy; The Priestess Code thanks you for your unwavering support. To the second midwife, Michelle Vandepas and her team, who are such a beautiful reminder that it takes a village, especially for a book.

Gratitude to my students who allowed these Principles to come to life, who reflected back the teachings, and who encouraged me with their deep desire to learn more about them.

Gratitude: to my parents who passionately raised me to seek what is Holy, without attaching labels.

Gratitude to my partner in life & love, Glen Cooper, who for the past nine years has entertained our spirited daughters while I wrote, edited, and sat in solitude.

To my girls: Dharma and Sarada. I owe you my life. You have given me direction, passion, and a deep desire to leave this world a better place for you. It is my hope and prayer that you and every woman who walks with you and after you get to do work that they love. This book is a seed we plant together so that more of us give ourselves permission to be our true self, and the world in turn gets to be blessed by such holy expression.

Introduction

$\mathcal{M}$ y beautiful initiate. You know there is something you are meant to be. Big things await you. At times, you feel clear where you are heading; other instances, you are totally confused how you ended up in this world that does not *get* you.

You feel the purpose of "who you are" knocking persistently at your door, though there are contradictions against your own intent: the desire of traveling, and the playfulness of having fun opposes the quietness that is awakening in you.

Uncertain of where you are headed, yet there is this nudging, a knowing that something big lives within you while simultaneously knowing you are here to experience life, to connect to the unseen loving forces you have begun to feel.

Coming to this place in life, it took treading rough waters to arrive while withstanding pain, a broken heart and disappointments. Yet amidst all that, you also see the magic. You see that a higher force calls you, and is making way for your unfoldment.

You are different than most, possessing a knowing that some seem to not understand or care to explore. You have wisdom beyond your years; however, finding words or a framework to be able to dwell within this space seems unattainable.

I am here to tell you that it is not unreachable. It will take practice, it will require for you to explore what it means to be awake. You need to push the boundaries of being in this world but not *of* this world.

I am here to make it easier for you to navigate life, to accept the ups and downs, the twists and turns, to find great pleasure in your journey. This is not necessarily a promise of an easy life. There will be moments where you will master challenges as well as moments where it will just feel damn hard. You will have nothing except the ability to ask for help, or choose to fall to your knees begging God to stop the pain.

Sharing that this too shall pass is not a cliché. I am here to provide a perspective, a road map of sorts, to make it easier on you in order to give you a leg-up in life. You will become the wise woman you already know you are, knowing exactly in what season you are and how to handle it. The tools necessary to not just overcome everything, but to create a life of fulfillment, happiness, and riches will be shared.

You will be held in these words. You will soften and be activated. These teachings that I am about to share with you will become your own. Take them into your heart. I promise that if you do that, even just one or two of these Principles will shift you into greater alignment with yourself, your path and all the beauty that you are here to create.

Allow yourself to settle into the knowledge that your life is sacred; everything you have and will experience is perfection. Perhaps it is not the kind of perfection you are used to imagining, but now is when we should speak of what it means to be a modern woman with bills and responsibilities, and one who is also curious to live a life in communion with Spirit (the Universe, God, Goddess, you name it - or not).

Yes, you can have your earthly cake and eat the heavenly manna that you so preciously deserve. You are a Modern Priestess.

In this book, I will lay out the Principles and Teachings that will help you with this endeavor and also share stories of women who crossed my path at Divine timing. Their personal stories will give you a sense of not being alone, knowing that women from all walks of life are Spiritual Warriors of their own lives.

I will admit that before this philosophy came into my life, I thought there was something wrong with me. My feelings were very intense, and I felt a lot of shame around my emotional ups and downs. Prior to my Presence practice (which will be shared in this book), I would try to control outbursts because I thought that I had to be in a constant state of peace to call myself a Priestess.

However, when I began to see that all my feelings were sacred as each had a message either showing me what was in alignment or showing me what needed attention to heal, the self-judgement slowly started dissipating. I had to make time to *feel the feelings* when I was alone. I practiced this for years, and now I am at the point where I can feel the uncomfortable sensations. Once the wave of emotions subsides, I could be present with the next fresh moment before me, without having the past (or past emotion) inform my reaction.

This takes practice and some discipline, but it is definitely doable to be honest about what we feel and be proactive about using the feeling to heal what is hurting within us, and even more profound to use all life experiences to bring us closer to what we desire. I no longer feel a slave to my feelings, but rather see them as a vehicle to being more aligned.

Although the context of the book is for women, I really feel that the healing and awakening laid out is less about gender, and more about the Feminine Essence we each possess. We all have masculine and feminine qualities, no matter if we are man or woman or someone on the gender spectrum. No matter your gender or sexual orientation, it is my hope that you find a home in The Priestess Code, the stories shared and your own journey.

Stories used by permission; some things have been modified and some names have been changed.

Table of Contents

Section One:

The Modern Priestess

Chapter 1

Concept of a Modern Priestess

A Priestess is a woman who feels ancient wisdom and connection to the Divine, with many manifestations of her devotion. She has spent lifetimes dedicated to the service of God (where you may interchange God for the word Spirit, Soul, Universe, Goddess, etc.) She feels a connection to her body as well as to the quiet moments, to nature, to yoga, to meditation, to sisterhood, to sex. She sees the sacredness of being alive and also deeply feels that holiness is inside her heart.

It has been painted as a notion that to be a woman of God, one must be pure, a virgin, have a servant's heart. We are told that women (such as Mother Mary or Mother Theresa) were infused by God's love though we know very little about their humanity. Mother Mary, or as she is called in Latin America *Virgen Maria*, was a woman first, yet everyone sees the holy woman, the virgin, the pure, the perfect mother, the mother of the Son of God. But is there more to her? Who is the woman entrusted with a holy man to raise. Who is the woman who birthed in persecution; who is the real woman behind the notion of a holy woman? My sense is that she was not much different than you or I; we, too, have access to such wisdom and love when we embrace the divine beings that we are.

Another example is Mother Theresa, a canonized saint who wrote letters to God about her humanness, on her depression and her struggles with God, her own service as well as the suffering of humanity she fought to cease. Akin to the circumstance of these women and what society has projected about who both are (or are not), we have faced the same constriction set by society.

Similar to these two women, there are many who oscillate from being fiercely devoted to the Divine to the other side of being transient with this relationship, but do not fit the mold of a woman of God (or at least the picture we have been painted a holy woman ought to be). We are neither nuns nor are living in ashrams; rather, we live regular lives with moments of being both Zen in addition to spicy. In fact, we love the zest of life. We love to laugh, to play; we love shoes, and love the most sensual of experiences life has to offer.

There are things that work toward peace, such as when we practice yoga, meditate and are devoted to growth, yet we are also very human. We may have felt guilty about our humanness, but our brilliant sensitivity offers us a possibility to see our sacred self, and denounce a self-deprecating view of ourself. I say to us that we are Priestesses, sacred women indeed. We may scream and fight, feel pain or command authority; we may withhold love. We experience the cycles of life openly, sometimes with tears, sometimes with comfort.

We are real and holy all at the same time. Know that you may say to yourself: I am a Priestess.

A Priestess has no box.

Do not question your journey, beloved Sister. There is no right or wrong decision. The only thing to do is to make a choice and make it right. Follow it, whatever it may be. Discover what you find sacred and dedicate your being-ness to that.

Love nature? Bless her with your presence; heal her and make her your temple.

Love commerce? Make that ground holy.

Love the idea of the path of motherhood? Do it with all you've got.

Love numbers? Help humanity embrace spreadsheets.

You decide. If your path is to jump from thing to thing and that makes you happy, keep at it, but first you need to make that a sacred path, too. If you decide to leave a legacy, dedicate your life, heart and actions to that which you love.

You have a voice. You may not know what that voice sounds like or for what it stands, but be relentless in your inner compass. Accept where you are, which could be a variety of stages such as you are single with no prospects, yet that is holy. Perhaps you have a partner and don't want children; then you must know that you are sanctified in that state of being. If you want marriage, family and Sisterhood, give yourself permission to be the next wave of feminist who makes all choices not only equally, but divinely.

Your past, your lineage and your desires dictate the direction of your life.

Concept of a Modern Priestess

Chapter 2

The Purpose of a Priestess

*W*hat is most precious about you is that your essence is your purpose. You are not about finding purpose in a job; you are about being purposeful in all that you do.

The paradigm of having a purpose define who and what you do is outdated. Rather, what is aligned with the evolution of Woman is that you focus on knowing who you are. That and only that will lead you to the riches of the most emboldened life. You *being you* is your ultimate purpose.

When you are in that seasoned time and age where you uncover the treasure that lies (and that has always been) within you, make it your practice to help another woman or man on their path. If this wholeness feels lifetimes away, assist a fellow Priestess with what you learn. Do it holding humility and value in balance as you watch the Universe thank you ten thousand fold.

Manage real life under the full moon.

A Modern Priestess has a life. She does not always have unlimited time to do yoga, meditate, get a massage and sit in silence every single day. She may be able to take one or two of these and prioritize them, but she has an active life!

You cannot expect just because you call yourself Priestess to do moon rituals every single month, bringing ceremony to every aspect of life. That is doable for the kind of Priestess who is fully and 100% dedicated to her spiritual path as a vocation. As a professional woman, you have networking events to attend, girlfriends to meet for dinner and a responsibility to yourself to nurture your spirit in whatever way fills you. Love to watch Netflix on a rainy Sunday afternoon? Do not judge what makes you happy; give yourself the gift of self-nurture.

As a Priestess who is a mother, you have big souls in little beings; your focus will look different than before motherhood. When your children are little, know that you are in the most challenging balancing act of life. Whether you work outside the home or care for these young ones full time, care for yourself also. Without you, the family is toast. Care for the valuable vessel of a coach and mentor that you are to those precious little ones. Become the queen of self-care, be known for that, inspire friends to do the same and model this lost art. You deserve it.

Chapter 3

Sovereignty in a Priestess

*T*he power of a Priestess is not defined by anyone, as when in her power, she has already proven that she can take care of herself as well as her loved ones and has more to spare. She knows that as a Priestess she is capable of standing alone, not necessarily needing anyone to sustain her.

Yet, she can choose to live accompanied not because she needs someone, but because she knows that she is powerful enough to be vulnerable to rely on another person. She understands interdependence while turning her back on co-dependency. She is not interested in people who are needy or who suck her energy dry. She is not interested in anyone else proving her own sense of value. She stands powerful on her own always knowing that her cup runneth over and from that place of being filled to the brim, she gives.

She knows when to share, the time to withhold and how to replenish. She is aware of her body, her needs and her desires. She responds to life from this solid place of knowing, fully feeling her feet planted and completely aware of her relationship to people and her surroundings. She vows to not keep herself small. She is free of guilt because she knows that part of her path is to trigger others into accepting their own power. This is not permission to be unconscious of other's feelings, but rather to give perspective on how our humanness allows evolution at a spiritual level, should they choose.

A Priestess in her power knows the land on which she stands matters, just as the community she chooses matters and she knows what is right for her in every moment. When things are not as clear, it is in those moments where either she closes her power thus losing her sense of connection or she forgives herself because she understands that forgiveness is power. When fully in her power, she takes 100% accountability for all that happens in her life. She does not do it in a self-mutilating way, but in a way that she accepts responsibility, understands the life teachings before her and makes a different choice.

This woman in her sovereignty knows boundaries. She knows when to say no. There are times when she knows that when she protects her energy and her domain that she protects the entire planet. A model of confidence, she is also completely aware that this strikes people in a different way. Some people receive it with admiration and others with disdain. Her confidence is easily misunderstood, but she remembers to have compassion for her fellow human travelers and continues to be herself.

She stops only if she has hurt someone. In that case, she helps her fellow sister, apologizes and makes a plan to do better. Her friend accepts the offering and the sisterhood deepens due to the challenge. A Priestess in her power knows that challenges make better people, and a Priestess also knows that growth is not always in the form of pain. Growth can (and does) happen with ease as well as grace, if she chooses to listen to her mind-body system. In her awakened state, she is both a step ahead and discerning of the soft prompts from life.

The power within the Priestess does not wait until she is fired from a job. She recognizes that gifted moment when her psyche drops the truth that it is time to move and she accepts the movement, takes steps towards the next phase, opens her arms to being upgraded in addition to expanded. She listens to the whispers of her soul when it is time to grow. She listens well, and she acts with confidence, with a sense of surrendering into her own self.

This type of Woman is not afraid of unexpected gifts in the forms of hard to understand illness, death, betrayal or a broken heart. She falls into the arms of her tribe, allowing herself to be human, to feel deeply, to be heard, to be held. Once the wounds are healed, she takes courageous moves to proceed with wisdom on her side. She does not play the blaming game, for she knows that each person is on their own journey and each person plays a role in the cosmic joke of life, yet she takes seriously those who surround her. She has high standards and that makes her embody compassion for herself, her very first love, which pushes her to choose a tribe that not only allows her humanity to rise in times of raw pain, but also holds a vision for her greatness and her incredible contribution to this home, our planet.

A Priestess in her power knows that circumstances do not define her; she defines the circumstances. Her feet planted, she determines the role of such a situation. She commands the right to say what she will and will not tolerate, with love because she is not afraid to love or to be loved. She blends into her partner as if heaven and earth were colliding in pure ecstasy. She knows she is different than her counterpart, but somehow the mix works, acknowledging the parts that do not completely work will allow the intertwining of the roots of trees to blend into one in time.

Patience is a product of time and she understands that she seasons, and that every single decade makes her a delicacy of life. She understands that every wrinkle, curve and contour defines the richness of a life well lived. Outside beauty does not define her, but she is not afraid to flaunt it, showing what she's got because she darn well pleases; nobody, not even cat callers, have the right to take away her profound power. Ever.

Chapter 4

Power of a Modern Priestess

*P*ower can mean so many different things to so many different women. When we talk about power, we are not talking about power over another person nor is it referring to power exerted on a situation to get what we think we need or want.

That is not true authentic power, but rather it is permission to be fully you. There is great fear in this, and that is normal. Emergence with any type of devotion to spirituality or personal growth carries great fear of rejection for many Priestesses, particularly as many are new to the understandings of the more sensual or sensitive side of being human. The ignorance of those who uphold the mind and suppress the senses (including the feelings) has dominated much of society; therefore, the Priestess has not felt safe for a long time.

Now things are very different. Yoga, meditation and spiritual growth movements have been modernized, working to some extent to normalize mind-body connection, mindfulness and spirituality. One very important fact for the Priestess of today is that it is safe for her to be who she is. Many who have come before her did not have this advantage. Just a generation ago being authentically feminine was taboo; quite frankly, in many parts of the world women are still fighting for the right to embody feminine qualities (using feelings, the sensual, the power of sisterhood) in life and business.

The struggle of balancing the feminine in the journey of every woman has impacted how safe the Priestess feels in expressing these qualities. However, times are changing and society is softening to new ways of being, demanding authenticity in existence. This is evident when we notice the gender and sexual orientation equality issues at the center of media and politics. Being uniquely you, without an exact box to check, is becoming more normal in modern civilization.

We cannot deny that the fear exists with this inclination to be different from the masses, one that incorporates a biological component. This is quite primal. If you think of a tribe setting, and the importance of being protected by the tribe, it becomes apparent why we have this instinctual need to belong. We are biologically programmed to care about inclusion.

What I am asking the Modern Priestess is to move into insight rather than only using instinct or old conditioning, and to begin practicing her natural way of being connected to her soul. The Priestess Code anchors the awakening, and balances the spirituality craved, and the practicality of being alive today.

A Priestess of today can access her power by choosing relationships that honor her, by negotiating work schedules that fit her desired lifestyle and by being in the world in a way that is aligned to her soul. It's all facets of living that lets her be able to take care of herself in every way.

Where do we give up our power?

Giving away our power hardly ever feels like an arduous war, where we would have surrendered after years of being beat down. Typically, giving away our power happens in little moments. It becomes a habitual pattern that takes over our lives until one day we realize we have slowly leaked our essence without ever realizing that it was not all intended for someone else. Through our power, we deserve to feed ourselves first and then humanity.

We all have stories of how we gave away our power and reasons why we were programmed to do so. The first Priestess I knew was a Latin American Catholic woman, who attended church, questioned the priest and fought with her neighbors to protect her land. But she also loved tenderly and spoke her truth. She was unlike many of her time. She had been married to an angry man who verbally abused her and tore up her precious photos of her children (perhaps his was less a story about anger and more of an unmanaged diabetic who wreaked havoc at home). As a good Catholic woman, she stayed through the birth of eight children, and then as the youngest turned five she left him in Venezuela during the 1940's.

A Priestess feels unsettled until she finds her temple, and this particular woman had none. She dedicated her prayers to her *Virgen Del Valle*, an apparition of Mother Mary in Margarita Island, off the coast of Venezuela, believing the *Virgencita* (as she called her) brought her back to Margarita to rest and live among her orchids and birds. This woman, my grandmother, Carmencita, represents the reclaim of power by the Priestess.

We may have given pieces of our power away slowly, one day realizing every relationship is off balance. Either we repair and heal what we have or we leave to forge new ground, recovering what was rightfully always ours to keep.

A Priestess, when re-gathering what had been lost, recognizes that nobody took "it" from her, but that she had been wrongfully programmed to over give, sacrifice or deny her own voice. Now that her eyes have been opened, she steps fully into her power while feeling her feet fully planted, understanding the strength of her core and knowing that unseen loving forces protect as well as guide her.

The Priestess reclaimed her power as an act of self-love.

The Lost Priestess

A Priestess of the Light loses her way from time to time. She has moments of getting caught in family issues, work deadlines, dating nightmares, children hurting, money problems, forgetting that everything in life is temporary and that solutions abound. Life happens to a Priestess.

This moment, or perhaps days or years of being a little off course, does not mean she is less powerful. It does not mean she has blocks. What it means is that a new path, a new way, a new paradigm awaits her.

First step to coming home to herself coupled with her inner light is to feel the essence of the turmoil, which is required in order to transcend it and forgive herself. If she does not, she will hold on to the temporary amnesia of her Light. The simplicity of the coming back to Self (the alignment of the light in her heart and the realness of her body in addition to her mind) takes practice. Coming back to the light and wholeness does not take much time, only a consistent heart and the simple reminders of how to be in Presence.

Presence is feeling connected, grounded and really alive. Eckhart Tolle beautifully explains in his book, *The Power of Now*, what it means to be in this state of being present in the moment. Being present is not void of feelings or void of sensuality. Being present is not about only being at complete peace. Presence is a verb. Presence has movement; it is dynamic and it is a vehicle offering self-healing.

Presence is available for all, and the Priestesses of this world have the most direct access to this power in her NOW. When a woman allows herself to feel, experience and absorb every sensation that arises, she is connecting to her truth in that sacred moment. What makes a moment mundane or void of grace is when we attach meaning to an uncomfortable feeling.

The process of self-healing is available. Ultimately, we do not need another person to heal us, bless us or voice the wholeness. We have access to this power. However, being supported by others, especially a group of women, is one of the most precious gifts a woman of the light can receive. In order to heal, we must make friends with our feelings, those powerful vessels of communication. Honoring them will not only do a lot of good, but will also allow for miracles to flow.

Feelings have important information to share. We have created lives where we respect and revere our thoughts as well as our mind, but we think very little of our feelings when, in fact, feelings have information that wants to be integrated. It's a force within, and thinking that we can mute only creates more pressure. You know what happens with pressure... too much, and an explosion follows.

So, how do we make peace with our feelings? Simple—feel them. When feelings are positive, it inspires increased alignment and happiness via an easy process. However, when the feelings are so overwhelming, hurtful and engrained in our most painful memories, it can be devastating. Seek support and advice from professionals who have the ability, knowledge and wisdom to encourage the healing process. Although you have the power to do this on your own, it does not mean that you have to do it that way. If the support is right, let yourself be courageous enough to receive help.

Whether using your own power or getting assistance, begin with small feelings and sensations. Begin practicing this Presence by practicing with small things, and when you feel you have the model for basic understanding, move to things that rattle your feeling of grounded-ness.

To heal yourself, I invite you to use Presence. I was first introduced to the concept by Eckhart Tolle in the book *The Power of Now* as I noted earlier, and then again via a method originated by Reinier Bosman as taught by Marieken Volz. Here is an example of how it works. When a thought or a sensation arises that triggers a negative feeling, focus on its sensation. For instance, if you are driving and someone cuts you off in traffic, you feel anger. Instead of blaming them or yourself, feel the sensation in your body to determine if it is localized somewhere specific by locating its vibration without labelling it, even almost forgetting that you labelled it.

This practice alone can relieve much of the stress in life. We place so much attention and energy toward the stressful things in modern life that freeing ourselves in this way, focusing on one way to process discomfort, creates a real opening for being more at ease, and hence more in the present moment.

This practice can be very disorienting at first because the mind and our own patterns are used to labelling stories, which ultimately creates suffering; it is a closed loop of feeling, labeling, stories, more feeling, more labeling, more stories, all increasing suffering.

The invitation I give to you through the Priestess Code is to feel the feelings, to begin your inner healing.

What is Presence to me is not Presence to you

Your experience of what it means to be "in the now" cannot be understood by another person or Priestess because it is unique. Become a detective as you start to get to know what helps you feel connected in the sensorial and visceral experience you possess. This allows your own version of connection, peace and perhaps even happiness.

Practice with the easy to feel feelings and then move to the more complex.

Chapter 5

A Priestess Has
Complex Feelings

You are feeling connected, grounded, really alive in your existence and suddenly a thought pops into your head about something you forgot (how you really miss your Beloved/family/sister/mother/dog). You focus on how you really should have brought them with you on your Caribbean get-away, generating guilt and voilà! Just like that, your mind starts racing, developing stories about how you're being an inadequate girlfriend, wife or mother. You start feeling anxious seeing all the couples, families and friends on the beach, completely questioning your decision.

Basically, you start going into a pattern we call suffering. All of that is real. That feeling that surfaced is not for you to push away, ignore or from which you should escape. It is real, and it is commanding that you hear that voice. Mastery is to acknowledge, feel and "let it rip" or flow through you. To develop mastery, it is important to be careful not to choose life-long pattern of feeling crummy about yourself or creating stories that support a derogatory pattern. Be gentle with yourself as you admit this cycle and still feel the feeling.

Have compassion and kindness for your process. Have patience for where you are right now. Remember you have lived this way your entire life and moving into "living in the NOW" will take some practice, but mostly it needs a willingness to receive what you feel at every moment as actually happening for you.

Your soul is indicating through the feelings what is real and what truth is for you, but it is also communicating the exact item that needs to be healed within. When this occurs, it is integrated more fully. This uncomfortable sensation is indicating something (most likely) ancient and likely is not the first time you have felt it. You are being guided by the Light through your own healing heart of what to feel and sense—allow it to run through your being.

When we allow the sensation to flow through us, we let energy run its course. The bigger the sensation, the bigger the need to allow it to surge. The more intense, sometimes it takes more time, but not necessarily. (This state of presence is your very own definition, and it is ever changing because you are ever evolving.) When you feel this wave, sit in silence; see if more sensation rises. After it subsides, it is time to let your creative power and energy emerge.

In our journey of attempting peace, we shove emotions aside in the pursuit of feeling good, which evades us because we (conscious or unconsciously) are wrapped in another frequency, another energy. How is it possible that peace can come to us when we are constantly in the stress of resolving what has remained open?

The path of the Priestess is one of acceptance (we will talk about this in the Principles later in this book). Acceptance of life, acceptance of what is, acceptance of where we are and deliberateness in the healing should be followed by the actions of creating a miracle filled life.

Miracles + The Power of Creation

The Law of Attraction has brought a great gift via awareness in our collective consciousness of our power to create. It has taught us that the mind is powerful and an important ally to having what we want. The Law has also reminded us that what we feel is really the motor to manifesting our desires into reality. The mind was wrong in seeing our perceived obstacles as blocks, and has missed the mark on acknowledging the journey we experience as sacred. Whether the material matches what we want or not, the life we have is sacred, good and right, all perfectly aligned.

The things we want in this material realm are momentary and transitory realities that we have the privilege to experience; they are not the juice of life. Things are momentary but the Priestess knows that the only thing that is the most aligned to her goal is her connection to the Light/ Spirit/ her Soul, and the manifestation on this planet is but the sweet aftermath. Understanding the experience on earth, especially as a woman is complex, gritty, and encased in much raw ecstasy, and allows the Priestess to be sacred in her humanness as well as in her holiness with her connection to the Divine.

When a Priestess is connected to her demi-goddess status, she is capable of using this power to materialize what she wants from this place of alignment. Here, she is connected to Womanesting™, the inclusion of Feminine Principles (and power) in materializing her desires. This occurs not only in the creative and manifesting process, but also in balancing both world and heaven in her essence. We undergo an evolution when we realize the value of the Femi-Feminine aspects, hence we WOMANest, rather than MANifest, bringing ourselves into Sacred Balance. A Priestess knows that when she is loving, creating, and connecting with her inner Light that she becomes more attuned to her true heart's desire. Through this approach, the inner plans of greed and desperation are eliminated, aligning her to a more authentic expression and hence a life that reflects her True Self.

Section Two:

The Priestess Code

Chapter 6

The Beginning

$\mathcal{T}$ he realities for being a Priestess require you face living both a life on earth and playing with the realm of the heavens by using a Code that can ease your earthly experience. This Code will balance the Law of Attraction's teachings, alleviate the stress of straddling two worlds and anchor an aligned solid path for the Priestess who is ready to live her purpose in a harmonious way. It is her natural gifts that make her ready to defy all the expectations that have been placed on her and now live fully in her power.

The Priestess Code bridges a gap between philosophies that are dichotomous and it asks us to choose happiness while ignoring all things that send us to reside in the abyss of our subconscious full time. The teachings within this Code are a way to honor the cyclical nature of human beings and still support our desire to be sustainable in a modern world. Even if we don't start with immediate understanding of The Code, we all return to the beginning until it is clear to us where we need to be, and that's actually how I finally understood its message.

The Principles within *The Priestess Code* came to me in a mystical experience… in the shower. It was a typical hyper-focused work day in my home office, and I paused mid-afternoon to shower before getting the kids from school. While showering I heard, *"Hold these Principles to be True and to live by."* My head spun, eventually making a 180 turn and then looking towards the ceiling. I had never had such an experience. I mean I had been talking to my angels as well as spirit guides, and recently really had connected to the spirit of the Divine Feminine, but the voice of my unseen loving forces always seemed to sound like a wiser version of myself. But this was different. This voice was not a part of a conversation I started; this message felt definitive, direct and ever so patient.

I grabbed a towel, water dripping everywhere and rushed to my bedroom to grab a pen. Looking up again, I said, "Ok, I'm ready." And one by one, the principles were dictated to me. I have printed them in this book—The Priestess Code and its Principles, their Truth and how they relate to our lives is written as a way for us to enter into the Balance of being alive, fully connected to the Divine. I remember writing them, staring at them, then thinking, "These are nice, but I don't live this way."

So I spent the next two years learning, breathing and integrating the first principle, *You are a Seasonal Being; Accept it.* I had no clue what that meant. I had been living a pretty masculine life of achieving, providing for my family and in a goal-hungry spiral. Not a cell in my body could comprehend that I was a seasonal being, and so I had to learn it intimately.

I tried to edit the various principles during the years, yet the original text would nudge its way back. Once I had a semblance of the first Principle, I moved to the next, and then the next. I deepened my understanding of each of them the best way I knew how: announce there would be a class, get people enrolled, and then two nights before the class I would write in the solitude of my husband's photography studio to receive the information that I would share. Because I understood that they were to be interpreted by each person, I would share what I knew, and then take each person into a meditation so that they could assimilate, integrate and make sense of them in their own way. It was important for me to share that they can receive them in whatever order they wished (i.e. more linear people could be sequential, but it was possible to start with the Principle that calls to the individual).

The point was also well established that the Principles are not mine, but are for each person to make their own, to ingest them with the appetite they desire to conjure and then use them to support each woman in the way that best fits her. Part of the process for me included interviewing women who paralleled the Principles shared in this section of this book, and then I sat on the writings for years. Not really knowing why, slowly the whole story of what it means to manifest as a Woman started coming into focus. This Code and the process of sharing it softened me in a way that not even Motherhood could have.

To embody Law of Attraction from a place of wholeness, so we may embrace our Feminine nature as is shared in the stories, is nothing new. Rather, it is a waking up to the power, nature and beauty of what it means to have alignment and balance with our Feminine and Masculine attributes is Womanesting™. Although not a secret, nobody speaks of this important quality in the realm of manifesting.

What I have discovered is that the Principles are a process. They are not separate; they work together. The dance of their play in our lives allows us to integrate their nature in a subtle way. The effects can be powerful, like a shocking awakening, but because of their wave-like energy, the process feels more like a gentle luring invitation into the depth of Divinity; when you are done, you realize that you are transformed, and that at the same time there is deeper and more intimacy to explore.

Happiness and fulfillment live with us when we quiet the mind, name the pain, deeply sense the pain, allow the wave of the sensation to take its course and continue to choose the present moment in alignment with The Light; the highest vibration possible. The cycles of our lives give us an opportunity to grow. We can grow in suffering or we can grow in authenticity with joy. I find that when each woman is clear on her purpose, the depleting effects vanish, and the more we affirm what we truly desire every moment (without denying what is real), then true abundance resides.

I realize now that The Codes are an engagement with the Feminine qualities of what it means to be a balanced being. As human beings, we have cycles (for instance, most everyone has heard of circadian rhythms, the cycles of sleep and awake) and denying cycles is out of alignment with our souls. This is why teachings in modern films or current books on the Law of Attraction fall short of giving people (particularly sensitive, soulful women) the ability to create a life in purpose, doing work that supports them and their families and also be nurtured by life itself. (Working with the cycles that will be described in this book, however, brings us to great peace, understanding and a systematic plan to move into a life full of purpose and authentic abundance.)

But I wondered how? How do we honor our individual story, honor who we are, create safe space for all women to tell their holy story with dignity, and move from that place into the next moment, where new stories are created from a blank slate and from a state of Presence?

The spiritual teachings by many of the modern day gurus (such as Deepak Chopra, Wayne Dyer, Eckhart Tolle and Abraham Hicks) provide beautiful wisdom, effective tools and were more or less working for me. I mean, I had manifested a year's worth of salary in a week, so I must have been doing something right, right? The teachings on manifesting invited me to get clarity of my desire, believe it to happen, take inspired action and I thought all would be peachy. If at any moment my emotions were not happy and optimistic, I discovered that I was essentially closing down the gates and blocking my desire. It gave me encouragement through some of these guru's teachings to *get happy* as often as possible, to follow my *bliss* and be mindful that all would be dandy.

However, the inner stories I was hearing from these women were not bringing me to a happy place; instead, they were taking me into a dark place in which I found myself struggling to escape. I did not have the appropriate tools or skill set to handle the pain that surfaced. *Getting happy* just felt like an insult to what we have gone through as women in our earthly experience. In my desire to get happy, I had forgotten about the sacredness and purpose of anger and sadness. If I got happy, what would happen to the women who were not, but who were getting release and healing in sharing their truth?

The choice to enter the dark portals was upon me, and I was confused. The laws of manifesting and Laws of Attraction were in complete contradiction to the sacredness of these women's stories and what they triggered within me.

Nobody seemed to have the answers. I was climbing the walls trying to make sense of the teachings from The Bible, Yoga Sutras, Buddhism, New Age movement coupled with the beautiful, powerful, real truth these women brought to me. I needed to understand how the two spectrums could co-exist in the world I wanted to create in my life, one of love, fulfillment and happiness. The Priestess Code became the missing link that harmoniously brought ancient and modern teachings together, and with it brought me more compassion to myself and others, and ultimately, more balance.

Now, after almost nine years of meditating on them and writing about the Principles, I breathe them, they breathe me. They are evolving every day for me. When I first received the Principles, I already knew intellectually that my life was off balance. I was able to recognize that the philosophy in the Principles could bring me to a more wholesome experience on this planet. I began with one Principle at a time in order to practice it, to use the philosophy and to apply it every day.

For instance, when I was practicing *You are a Seasonal Being; Accept it,* I forced myself to explore how I felt on any given day, to name the inner season and to learn to accept that each season had value in my life. Another example was when I explored *Connect to a Sisterhood; it will Strengthen you,* I forced myself to steer away from my natural tendency to tackle problems alone, but rather make myself vulnerable to receive help.

Through the years, I have practiced all the Principles. Some I feel I have mastered, and with some I am still a student. I feel these Principles came to change me, and as they helped me feel more connected to my life, career, family and myself, I could see that others could benefit from embracing the Feminine nature they bring.

The more I share them, the more that awakens within me. The women who are now exploring these principles have made it their own, too. This book is less about educating us on the components of The Code and is more an introduction to *The Priestess Code's* Principles to allow each person to explore for themselves.

The Beginning

Chapter 7

Seasonal Being

Principle: You are a Seasonal Being;
Accept It.

*W*e have been taught to achieve, move up, accomplish goals; we have not been shown how to accept, weather and benefit from the times when life does not look as predictable. Nobody can prepare us for those moments when having kids comes sooner than expected, when a job derails a career path or when a loss stops us dead in our tracks—until now.

This principle will prepare you for each year, the theme that follows you on any given year and the tools to utilize for your long term success in life as well as business. This particular instruction helps put things into perspective. As a human being, and especially as a woman, it is natural to see that life does not always unfold the way we plan. Understanding the yearly cycles is helpful, but also having patience and trust creates the attitude that life is happening for us, not to us.

Let me explain how this reality unfolded in my own life by using the Principle. When this principle first came to me, I was living a very masculine, linear manner, moving up the corporate ladder. Frustration would rise as I looked around at others and saw the success they were having. Although I noticed my own gifts, I didn't really understand why I was not achieving what I wanted financially, professionally and in my close relationships.

I was not aware at the time that I saw success as a linear path involving fancy titles and a growing net worth, but the wisdom (in fact the truth of being a seasonal being) brought more depth to the experience of being a woman in a complex modern world. Deprogramming myself from what I thought was a logical path in my career and re-programming my life to see the value of all the seasons, including stillness.

The Seasons

First I looked to the seasons in nature as a way to better understand its gifts.

Spring: a time of opportunities, the energy of Yes! represents the color and beauty of flowers, listening to birds enjoy the warmer days, observing as the rain nurtures the green.

Summer: a time to enjoy, rejoice, gather with friends, go to the ocean, have parties, bond as a family.

Fall: gathering the harvest, return to being productive, marvel in the color change of the leaves, begin to focus more intently on business.

Winter: inner time, to write, to reflect, to look back at the entire cycle and plan for the next planting.

When we see the full cycle of the seasons, we can better understand that each contributes to the entire process of creation. Some of the seasons are harder to be *in* and tougher to integrate what is going on in our lives, especially when it does not match the outer season. Inwardly, it may feel as though we are having a wintery day, but outside the sun is shining bright, causing us to feel guilty that our inner landscape reflects very little of what we observe in the world outside of our head and psyche.

Radically accepting what is present both inside and outside is the beginning of a life lived with peace as our ally. The first step to healing is to accept who we are, what we feel in both our past and present moments. Only then can we move into a different cycle. As human beings, the changes in season and cycles is inevitable, but how we navigate the changes is what separates us from suffering and allows stepping into conscious thriving.

Take for example our reaction to winter. Not accepting the winter within is common. We have been taught to suppress the shadow aspects, the darkness, to shine light on that which makes us uncomfortable with happy thoughts and affirmations. All of those strategies are good and helpful in coping with the complex lives we live, but when we ignore the healing that is surfacing, that is when we get into trouble. By burying it, one day all of that explodes in our face. Accepting the enjoyable seasons is also sometimes challenging for some of us; we feel guilty for the blessings before us or hold an expectation of a change in the course of our happiness. Yet radically accepting, experiencing and basking in the energy of the blessing allows for us to open to bigger blessings.

The principle of seeing life as seasons is a feminine concept aligned with nature. It is based on the wise understanding that life has ups and downs, twists and turns. Life is intended to have an element of mystery with a tad of messiness to nudge us into growing and digging a bit deeper than what most experience.

The path of the Priestess is understanding how she fits into the seasons and what her season is on any given day in order to support herself more authentically.

Nine Star Ki

The most powerful tool that I know on how to align a Priestess to her natural yearly cycle is looking at Nine Star Ki.

Nine Star Ki (*Ki* is the Japanese word for *energy* or *life-force*) is one of the oldest forms of astrology still used. This system is connected to the book of the I Ching, which is also responsible for other Eastern teachings such as acupuncture and Feng Shui.

This Ancient system helps us to understand the constant changes that make up our lives. If you really think about it, everything in life is in flux—*in constant motion*. Life is made up of seasons, of calculated and gradual changes. Measuring these changes allows us to better understand our behavior, and helps us prepare for what lies ahead.

The Nine Star Ki is a branch of Chinese Astrology that believes that energy is constantly moving. As Einstein said, energy cannot be created or destroyed. The Chinese believed that energy constantly alternates between two extremes: yin (female energy) and yang (masculine energy.) What this means is that there are specific periods of your life where you will be yin (contracting and gathering) and periods where you will be yang (growing and expanding). This is continuously going on in your life, whether you are aware of it or not. The key is to be aware of it and to work with nature, instead of against it.

This system focuses on five energy elements: water, soil, wood (tree), fire, and metal. Each element represents a different stage of your life. Using Nine Star Ki can help determine where you are energetically, and what the most appropriate course of action will be on any given year.

The cycle starts with (1) water, which is internal, then continues into soil in preparing the ground with (2) soil. As it begins to move it goes upward forming the tree energy (3 tree and 4 tree) then allowing time to rest in (5) soil. Then, it begins to form into solid, yang (6 and 7) metal. Pausing again at an introspective (8) soil. Next, it gets to its hottest point, which is (9) fire. Finally the energy transforms back into (1) water, where it repeats the cycle.

Each calendar year represents one of nine numbers in the Nine Star Ki system. Your unique cycle on any given year is determined by your birth date. Knowing these cycles is also important to help you understand how to plan your career or business year after year.

The more you know about what your year looks like and what the focus ought to be, the better you can understand what you need to do in order to find the greatest success. Some years your focus should be placed on family or health and other years the focus is financial opportunities. In (9) fire years (for example) the time is ripe for publishing a book, and getting your message out there on a grand scale.

In Nine Star Ki is there are three numbers: Primary Number, which is our general characteristic, Character Number which is our energy during childhood and who we revert to under pressure and stress, and Energetic Number, which is the energy we reflect out into the world. To determine the yearly cycle, for simplicity sake, we only look at Primary Number.

YOUR PRIMARY NUMBER CAN BE DETERMINED BY USING A SIMPLE FORMULA:

1) Take the last two digits of your year of birth, and add them together.

 IF the sum is 10 or greater, then add these two new numbers together to come to a single digit.

2) Subtract this digit from ten. The difference is your Primary Number.

Note: The Nine Star Ki year begins around February 4th or 5th, the point between the Winter Solstice and the Spring Equinox. People born before this date have a Primary Number of the year before.

9 Fire	8 Soil	7 Metal	6 Metal	5 Soil	4 Tree	3 Tree	2 Soil	1 Water
1910	1911	1912	1913	1914	1915	1916	1917	1918
1919	1920	1921	1922	1923	1924	1925	1926	1927
1928	1929	1930	1931	1932	1933	1934	1935	1936
1937	1938	1939	1940	1941	1942	1943	1944	1945
1946	1947	1948	1949	1950	1951	1952	1953	1954
1955	1956	1957	1958	1959	1960	1961	1962	1963
1964	1965	1966	1967	1968	1969	1970	1971	1972
1973	1974	1975	1976	1977	1978	1979	1980	1981
1982	1983	1984	1985	1986	1987	1988	1989	1990
1991	1992	1993	1994	1995	1996	1997	1998	1999
2000	2001	2002	2003	2004	2005	2006	2007	2008
2009	2010	2011	2012	2013	2014	2015	2016	2017
2018	2019	2020	2021	2022	2023	2024	2025	2026

General characteristics of each number are as follows:

1 Water: Represents the different flow of water and the journey of life. This person is as expansive as the ocean, as flowing as a river, and sometimes as murky as the dark waters. This is a person that can range in all these expressions and is probably connected spiritually in some form or another.

2 Soil: Represents Partnership or Marriage. This person has a characteristic of fertile soil primed for planting. This is the person that is a Mother archetype energy and deeply craves & thrives in community.

3 Tree: Represents the energy of Family, spring, and young shoots. This is an energetic person. One who is always moving and who is always exploring opportunities, but not always fully planted in one.

4 Tree. Represents the energy of Wealth and Prosperity. It is the oak tree archetype; roots planted, tall, but can be seen as swaying in the wind. This person can be planted but also can go with the wind and change their mind often.

5 Soil: Is the archetype for Yin/ Yang symbol, of the balance. It is the person that can see all sides, and has difficulty in uprooting.

6 Metal: Represents Father archetypal energy. This person is a great communicator and can appear more rigid yet carrying authority. This person carries an aura of authority and leadership.

7 Metal: Represents creativity and child-like fun. This person can adapt easily and has a magnetic and creative characteristic.

8 Soil: Is represented in the Mountain. This person seeks knowledge and perhaps depth and spirituality.

9 Fire: Represents Fame & Reputation. No matter what, this person is always noticed when they walk into a room. They are energetic, but can tend to burn out at times.

Yearly Cycles:

To simplify the calculation to know what yearly cycle you are in 2017, you would add +4 to your Primary Number to determine the cycle for the year. So, if you are 1 Water, you would be in 5 Soil House in 2017. If you are 8 Soil Principle Number, you would be in 3 Tree House in 2017. In 2018, you would add 5 to your Primary number to know your cycle or House. This pattern continues for the years to come: 2019, add 6.

This House cycle determines the energy that is most supportive for this year. A very basic description of the energies that support each year are as follows. I like to use the analogy of planting a garden to describe much of these energies.

1 Water House: It is a very Yin year. It is a foundational year in the nine-year cycle. It is a time when most people start a family or have recently changed their course in life or career. It is a time to be internal, to focus on spirituality, and a time to envision the next nine years. A time to plan out the garden. I always advice a Priestess to see this inward year as sacred and foundational.

2 Soil House is a time of preparation and the initial implementation of the plan. The activity seems more internal and not necessarily obvious to others, but it is a good time to prepare for what is ahead. Perhaps building the gate for the garden, preparing the soil, planting seeds, watering. I recommend to my clients to have patience during this year and remember they are building something for long term.

3 Tree House is a year of opportunities. It is a time where shoots start to show. I call this the year of *YES* and it is a very Yang year. I recommend when people are in this year to take more risks and explore more outward activities, but to also prepare their support system and family for the very active year.

4 Tree House is still a year of growth, but more of discerning what opportunities from previous year you want to water. It is

a year to focus in on what crops are bearing fruit and perhaps letting go of the crops that are taking up too much energy. In some ways this is the year of *No, thank you*; where we discern what is and is not working, and we courageously choose what truly feeds us.

5 Soil House is a year of Balance. An ideal time to practice self-care, self-nurture, and can have an inward focus. The previous two years have been active, and this is perfect time to stop and re-access where we are going. Often I encounter powerful women struggling to accept the stillness of such a year, but I have yet to see a Powerful Priestess not benefit from such a healing year.

6 Metal House is a year of Harvest and Leadership. It is a time when we are noticed from a career and business stand points. Promotions and growth are common. Perfect times to seek new employment or publish a book, as authority and leadership qualities are apparent. I often counsel women to prepare this time of stepping into their area of mastery.

7 Metal House is one of creativity and fun. It is an aspect of harvest that is more celebratory in nature. It is a year where I usually recommend that a Priestess treat herself to having more fun, to exploring their creativity, and to letting themselves be more child-like.

8 Soil House is one of stillness and strength. It is a good time to learn something new or in more depth. It is also a good time to focus spiritually in a more inward nature. I usually recommend this time as ideal to learn to meditation, read more, and follow their instincts in what will deepen their connection to themselves and Spirit.

9 Fire House is one of fame and recognition. It is a time when we are noticed more, and a culmination of the 9-year cycle. It is good to prepare for such recognition, and to take the

lessons from the cycle to bring wisdom to decisions. It can be a time when many women can feel burned out if they do too much, so pacing themselves is advised. Whatever has been cultivated for the entire 9-year cycle comes to fruition, and foreshadows of what internal work you will do the following year, will become apparent here.

The best use of this information is to plan for the energies that support us. No matter if it is a yang or yin year, support is important for a Modern Priestess. If it is a year of more inward journey, prepare your loved one, and your bank account. If it is a year of opportunities and much movement, it is a good time to set up support at home and also support in preparation for expansion in career, business and net worth.

Relationships

I have spoken to women who have been married for decades and what I have found is that they experience seasons in their relationships; ups and downs, and accepting and navigating the changes, and coming back together is what allows each of them to evolve as individuals, as a couple, and as a unit.

The ebb and flow of relationships can really be felt the longer you are with someone. There are moments in romantic relationships where things are good, solid and fun; then there are times when we ask ourselves why would we ever choose such a partner, we question our sense of happiness and fulfillment and romanticize options of escaping alone or finding someone else.

What I have seen in my 16-year marriage has been that the willingness to hold space for another as they navigate through their seasons and being held when the rockiness or the highs of life unground us creates a dynamic of support and longevity. Accepting the seasons someone else is living and not taking their inner or outer struggles personally creates a sense of trust in ourselves, in another person and in the relationship itself.

Patience through the different seasons is understanding that joy is not about only highs and happy moments, but about ruthlessly accepting where you are, where they are and where the relationship is. As Willa Cather said *Where there is great love there are always miracles.*

Love is the unifying force that keeps a relationship withstanding the change of seasons. The uncompromising love in ourselves is what allows us to stay awake for when the relationship is no longer serving our highest good. Sometimes ends are important in order for a woman to evolve and become her most embodied aligned Priestess self. Every woman has a unique path on this planet, but I have found that a universal truth is if those in our lives support our spiritual development, then they belong in our space; if they do not, we have decisions to make on either creating space between our dreams and their influence, or saying goodbye.

A Priestess and Her Career

Whether a Priestess is employed by an institution (Corporation, Government, Non-Profit, Academia) or is self-employed is secondary. Most Priestesses have a sense of wanting to serve something greater than themselves, and they will find a path that best supports them to achieve this desire. But sometimes we confuse our own identity with the jobs we have; we can correct this with a shift in perspective to bring us more peace on our purposeful path.

As a Priestess, it can feel that our career or business is one with us. It is true that we affect our job or business, but we are not *it*. We have a soul. The business has its soul. This truth can liberate you and empower you as well as your mission, and appropriately place your career/business in your experience.

We feed that soul, and the career/business' soul feeds us; it is a symbiotic relationship and a co-creative process. Keeping the separation can be challenging, but treating ourselves and the career/business as two separate entities gives us space to be introspective for our changing seasons. It is a way to be pragmatic and systematic with the cycles of our career/business. Like any relationship, it is about giving and receiving in balance.

I have heard it spoken that women do not climb corporate ladders; rather, we climb corporate monkey bars. This reflects the pull we feel to do well in our work, take care of family and establish wellness in our own personal lives. A way to help find balance appropriate for our soul is Nine Star Ki. It has been an incredible resource and tool to ground me into the season being experienced in my career.

We are trained to grow, grow, grow—what happens if our career/business is not in that trajectory and some years there is slow down? Does that mean that the work is a failure? I don't think so. Life has its ebb and flow, and so too do the ways we earn our monies; it has a separate soul and unique mission to fulfill. Some years it is about pausing and making decisions that affect the next nine to ten years, whereas sometimes it is about saying yes to all opportunities. Perhaps it means for you a year to go within yourself and write a book; some years may be about reaping the rewards of years of work and becoming famous or receiving a well-deserved promotion.

Careers and businesses have cycles and seasons. Accepting and most importantly understanding these cycles is paramount to continuing to usher and support success.

Seasonal Being

Chapter 8

Deconstruct and Construct

Principle: Deconstruct and Construct;
it is your Nature.

 ransitioning from one season to another is intended to
hurt a little, but it can feel good too, like the sore mus-
cle feeling post workout. The process of having to adjust to a
new season, a new circumstance or an ending is challenging to
most of us. Yet this challenge or pain can be perceived very
differently than an experience of suffering. Change is inevitable in life (and business, especially for a Priestess); nature
shows us this year after year, season after season, day after
day.

Frankly, if life remained the same we would become
bored and miss the opportunity to grow, to become more
whole, to embody and experience true joy. But somehow we
dread change. We have been conditioned to avoid pain and to
turn away from anything that may represent confronting the
uncomfortable parts of being human. We are afraid of the
dark, look away from facing the grittiness of life, and some-

times we even do all we can to escape the reality of our hurting heart.

I have done shadow work (which is when you scan through all the inner blocks and dig up all that is painful in order to heal), but I do not see that as *the* answer. I do not see the answer to constantly dig for what is dark, unhealed or blocked within us as the most efficient path in life. I think it leads us astray from why we are here on this planet, and it derails us from seeing the beauty in this world, including ourselves. Retrospection and introspection are necessary to evolve, but I do not think we have to spend a life uncovering darkness within ourselves. However, I do not condone denial as it is a journey of burying things that only explodes at the most inopportune times, or ends up being unfavorably manifested in our bodies and life.

The dark night of the soul types of transformation are a very compelling because sometimes the darkness can swallow us whole, making us think there is value and nobility in dragging ourselves through the mud of our personal underworld. When we suffer, we lose ourselves in darkness and await for light to surface at the end of the dark tunnel.

We have all gone through personal hell. I know this is necessary for some of us, but it is only one potential path. I recognize that at times in life (and business) we have no control of what arises, and although these hard situations can be incredible teachers, they are not the only way for us to grow. If darkness has become your way to grow, have compassion for yourself. Love yourself through it and ask yourself whether you feel ready for a new way of breaking through your own personal expansion and growth.

Another path to transformation is to enter into a pragmatic, yet lusciously real tunnel of acknowledging what needs to end, pausing to mourn, gain clarity of next step and then creating what is new.

What is Deconstruct?

Deconstruct **is about having courage to say goodbye.** It is about having the clarity in timing when a previously acceptable structure is no longer suitable to what we desire in life. Tearing down this structure is the next logical and most compassionately act of self-love.

This Principle about deconstruction involves tearing down a house to rebuild one that is safe, appropriate, more beautiful, more aligned and gives us room to grow. We realize a house has to be torn down for various reasons. It has mold or the structure is collapsing, for instance, and we either ignore it or do something about it. Perhaps it is the home where we were raised, but there are memories upon memories hidden in the walls of this place we called home. Yet, it must come down.

We cannot help ourselves feeling as though we are losing a loving member of our family. It could be that the home has become so toxic that every moment spent there is a reminder of the damage it has caused—we choose to feel trapped or to liberate ourselves from it. Deconstruct is about choice and it is also about growth, liberating ourselves from the oppressive mark of a horrific past.

Deconstruct is about how powerful we are in the choice to destroy what no longer serves. It is about accessing the spiritual warrior nature from within ourselves, among the tribe that surrounds us and accessing the trust that we are making the decision that is tough while necessary as the Priestess. It's important to know there are differing approaches to *deconstruct*. Some people prefer to take the whole house down with a bulldozer and be left with an empty lot. Others prefer to remove one room at a time, slowly adjusting to the change. There is no right or wrong approach to deconstruct, only the one that is most supportive for the woman.

A Priestess understands that she is ever evolving and that her warrior nature demands that she let outdated things - beliefs, relationships, personas, circumstances, jobs, partners, business models - go. She evolves; therefore, she has the power to face the challenge of endings, frequently disguised as feeling afraid.

We all have this "friend" called fear. She sits with us, especially in those moments when we know we must change, but are apprehensive to the impending results. Fear is normal, natural and human. It originates in a part of our brain that wants to keep us safe, protected and alive. She is primal, with access only to part of our brain, but she can rule, if we let her loud voice take charge.

We have the power to co-exist, crush, or put her in her place with the perspective that we are more than a response to outer stimulus. Our outside reality does not always reflect the power we have inside. Sure, it is nice to have the outside be peaceful, graceful and easy. If it is not, it does not mean that we have to choose to mirror caos, fear or anxiety. We have the power to re-direct life. We have the power to message ourselves and the Universe to take ownership of whom and what we are, to say what we want. Fear does not get to do that unless we let her.

The path of transformation asks that we access our power and place fear in her proper place. She has warned us, we have heard. It is taken into consideration the information she provides, and then we access our full brain, our full heart and our full soul to be willing and able to facilitate the Deconstruct. Fear is also an indicator that our human side is not in agreement with our spirit side, and so the strong emotion indicates that our perception of the situation before us is at odds with Universal truth. This does not mean to ignore instinct, but an opportunity to open ourselves to the litmus test of noticing what our system is communicating to us.

Deconstruct: The Process

The What

The path of the Priestess is one of evolving. She knows in her heart when is time to leave a job or a partner, change her business model, fire an employee, buy a car, get the boots, hire the intuitive, marry her partner, book the retreat… but she either listens or ignores herself and her heart.

Either way, the change is coming. She gets fired, worse things happen with the partner, clients leave all at once, the troubled employee steals the list of customers, the car breaks down, snow falls; she goes back to the old boots, she feels more lost in life, the guy/ gal decide they cannot wait anymore. The Universe/ God/ Soul gives us nudges for the decision or the change that must happen, so we minimize the message to no avail. The message comes on stronger, hitting us over the head with a two by four. We could have avoided the pain, but somehow we love torture.

Or we decide to listen to the nudges every time, to keep our eyes open to the prompt of the soul. The Priestess does not always have to know the details of what is about to change, but to some extent it is important that she bring consciousness and awareness of what is to change.

The Speed

It is important to remember that we have a say (sometimes!) on how quickly the change occurs. Speaking from the mind and from a bit of impatience, most of us want things to change quickly, but the truth is that the system does not always do well with ripping off the old band aid. Some systems thrive in slow and steady versus fast and furious. Knowing ourselves is key in knowing what and how we can handle the shift.

The Support

The seasoned Priestess no longer negotiates self-care and support; she has it built-in because she takes responsibility for her growth and up leveling. She has compassion for herself when she forgets, but she ensures her nurturing support is in place. She has the wisdom to know she cannot do this alone because that change will take its toll on the nervous system as well as physical body, so she readies herself to care for the basics.

My favorite go-to support during transformation is regular chiropractic care. I also choose to float in a deprivation tank, indulge in my nightly Ayurvedic dry brushing, get ayurvedic massages, take candlelight showers, immerse in magnesium or sea salt baths, or spend a day to read or watch movies. Basically, whatever allows my system to decompress, unplug and align, that's what I'll do. When I forget to bring wellness into my life, my body always seems to remind me and nudge me to take care of myself.

The Pause

It is very easy to tear down a house and start building right away, thinking that we know what we want. Yet, I urge a pause because in the magic of silence, pure brilliance unfolds. Sitting in stillness is a gift we have not learned to give ourselves or been taught its importance. The Priestess knows it is time to bring the pause and silence back to trend. She dances in the stillness with patience. Even when her mind races, she brings herself back to how important this silence is for the unfolding of what is next. She knows that in the silence, the soul speaks.

When a Priestess forgets the power of such silence, she learns to quiet her mind and drop into surrender. My friend Karen Curry Parker has a method of calming the mind and surrendering that she calls Seed Statement. It is a gentle tapping on the pineal gland (third eye that lies behind the point between the eye brows) and saying to yourself as you are prepared in silence to listen, "What needs to be released, healed and aligned for me to (fill in the blank).

Clarity and Intention

Clarity is the result of the pause. One moment we are mourning the loss of what was and the next moment (in the midst of the silence), the clarity moves us off the couch and into action with more vision and energy than we could imagine possible. The wait can be tough, but the clarity is so sweet and aligned, diminishing fear, perceiving less obstacles, connecting to hope and knowing that although we do not know the details, the next move feels right from the gut.

The energized feeling of knowing and the clarity of direction can quickly take over the plan of what house to build. (Before drafting the new plans, I recommend setting an intention for what this house will hold.) The new construction is a representation of what is next in our lives or with our work. As the symbol of the new direction, it merits clarity of intent in choosing the essence. For instance, if you are going to decide to change your career or business and you have clarity for what is next, pause and set the intention for what you truly desire in the next phase. Consider what truly aligns to you, to your profession and to those you serve. Be clear and intentional, and then take action.

The power of intent is underestimated, but the ease of decision making follows when we are clear of the new phase of life, be it living in a home or upgrading our business. The Priestess understands that all changes in life (whether personal, spiritual, healing or business related) affect her cause and she creates space in her life to honor those changes. However, the abundant Priestess sets systems in place to ensure that her work thrives even when she is taking down time. She implements a business model that supports her from financial stand point, no matter what is going on in her personal life.

If she finds herself not being able to do this, she deserves to deconstruct and negotiate for a role that supports her ever-evolving spiritual landscape. Negotiating a work model that allows each of us to blossom is important not just for our personal evolution, but important to the next wave of a Feminist movement that brings more balance to all people.

Chapter 9

Highest Form

Principle: You are here to be the Highest Form of who you are and nothing else. Love that.

O ne of the most appropriate phrases when I think of this principle is from the Dali Lama: *"The purpose of our lives is to be happy."*

We have been taught to have a plan, so much so that a "day planner" is part of our ritual into adulthood and corporate society. Other plans include New Year's resolutions, Five Year Plans, Ten Year Plans, Business Plans, Retirement Plans and even Vacation Plans. Everything is planned and executed as close to the plan as possible. Then life happens, and well, the plan mostly gets thrown out the window as we do everything we can to survive and should we dare, thrive.

As we contemplate the list of *shoulds* we have for the day, we glimpse the intense judgment and expectations we bring into life. We have ideas (mostly super imposed by our parents, society, or our past) and we muddle through life trying to accomplish, achieve and win the game. Most of us make very little room for quiet space, for getting to know ourselves more intimately.

Instead, everyone wants to move. Action is revered in our culture, and it's true that there is a purpose as well as place for it. We travel down the journey of life and a path appears where we consciously choose to move in the direction of that path or choose to follow another. The Universe wants us to take action, so much so that when the silence is present, the activeness within each of us can move with the inspiration presented to us.

Even finding our *Life Purpose* becomes a task, making the organic nature of uncovering our gifts and passions stumped and stifled. Our life purpose is to be. As we *be*, the inspiration and action move us into a direction of purpose whether it is for the purpose of one week, one month, one year, ten years or of a lifetime. The ever-evolving nature of Life suggests that a static purpose would not serve our thirst for growth and evolution. To fixate on one job per lifetime may be limiting, and may actually lead us into an unfulfilled life; if we do not experience fully who we are, it is a tragedy.

With every Principle, hidden in the words is an action to take. Even if we feel that a particular Principle invites us into the quiet of the *being* the action is to fall in love with ourselves. Take, for instance, falling in love. It means to be uninhibited, vulnerable, trusting, allowing and knowing that we are supposed to be exactly where and who we are. There is no *doing* aside from that *being*. When we enter into a new relationship, we enter into a vortex of potential, but it is difficult to maintain this vortex between conditioning, belief systems, stories we tell ourselves or stories others tell us. We are brilliant at reasoning why it could not be true love or we start searching for reasons to un-love this person.

This is withholding. As we withhold, we take away our chance to see Heavenly love clearly. To counter this with your Presence, you need to remember to take a deep breath and acknowledge where you withhold, take a minute to breathe it out of you so that you can remember how you want to love. What is beyond the love we feel for ourselves and the compassion of accepting where we are is the continuous devotion to growing. The devotion for raising our vibration, for taking ownership and responsibility for our own happiness is in our hands. Making decisions of whom and what surrounds us brings us to a higher state of love - self-love, universal love, heavenly sacred love.

Raising Our Vibration

Life happens for us, not to us. It happens for us to bask in the goodness and beauty of what surrounds us. We all know that there are certain people who drain our energy, who are unconscious or conscious energy vampires, absorbing the happiness right out of us.

Most people have a certain amount of energy to exert. (Of course if we tap into Universal energy, we have unlimited energy.) In order to be tapped into this boundless energy, we have had to practice this connection, which is a wave with ups and downs. It is important in order for us to raise our vibration to know our starting point and where we are at any given time. This saves us from being sacrificial and depleting our inner resources. It also awakens our consciousness to know when we can give, when it is vital to receive, when it is important to retreat and when it is ok to take action.

As a Priestess, knowing when we need to receive and when we can give helps us manage our day, our relationships, our social life, our self-care, etc. As a Merchant Priestess (aka

Entrepreneur or Corporate Leader), knowing the fullness of our energetic bucket lets us know when our energy is available for projects, negotiations, networking, marketing and selling.

When we understand the amount of energy we have on any given day, it affects our decisions. If there is a toxic person with whom we need to interact, we can better manage it by taking extra care of ourselves or knowing when it is appropriate to be around them (and when not). In the same token, when we know we are overflowing in energy, it is wonderful to capitalize by solving problems, pouring it into completing projects or having tough conversations because we know that we are centered enough to handle it.

Three tools that I have used to work with my vibration have been following the cycle of the moon, paying attention to mercury retrograde and my own menstrual cycle. These factors help me manage my sensitive energy as I play within my personal and professional life.

Cycles of the Moon

I find that as Priestesses, we are very much affected by the moon via her energetic pull and her cyclical nature. We only have to look at the ocean tides to know that the moon affects water; given that our bodies are composed of approximately 55% water, we can intuit that there must be some biological effect. The new moon is the perfect time to connect to the intellect and intentions; the full moon is time to allow the feelings and release to be a monthly practice. There are other aspects of lunar effects, but this is the basic monthly rhythm on which Priestesses can sync with the wisdom of nature. The moon really serves as a mirror to our ever changing feminine nature, and when she is honored, a part of us is also honored.

Mercury Retrograde

Mercury is the planetary influence associated with communication. When it is in retrograde (its perceived orbit in relation to Earth is going "backwards"), it tends to affect all communication, from electronics, personal discussions, contract negotiations and even inner self-talk.

A Priestess capitalizes on mercury retrograde by being internally focused, withholding from controversial conversations, pausing on negotiations, not signing contracts. Mercury retrograde is a good time (usually there are several of these per year) to be observant of one's own life, to take all that arises inside in order to contemplate and to heal.

Mercury Retrograde is also an auspicious time to complete unfinished projects. It can be a powerful time to stop all outward momentum in order to finish what we started in the past. As an example, I have used most Mercury Retrogrades to work on this book. The zig zag nature of being a Modern Priestess can derail us from projects, and having a few times a year when we can plan to return to what matters the most is very useful!

Menstrual Cycles

Our bodies are perfectly orchestrated to guide us through life. The belief that our cycles are flawed or that they are a punishment of some sort is an outdated patriarchal notion that women are not sacred. Our cycles are the reminder every day that there is life, there is choice and there is death. We live it and even before and after we menstruate, we are connected to this through our Priestess and Woman lineage.

Suzanne Mathis McQueen has the best book (*Four Seasons in Four Weeks*) on how to utilize our cycles as a compass to commune with nature and negotiate our way through living in society as well as engaging in business. The wisdom is within, and if we pay attention to how our energy relates to our cycle, we can plan our lives accordingly. For instance, if we feel tender and sensitive at a specific time in our cycle, we would not plan to lead a big event. Of course, we cannot always predict important meetings or backpacking vacations by trying to align them to our menstrual cycle, but it is during those days that it is important to introduce extra self-care, to be softer and gentler with ourselves. It may mean giving ourselves the day off if we need to recharge and honor where we are.

As Priestesses, raising our vibration is about managing the inner and outer realities and choosing Light as much as humanly possible. We need to ignore what is a distraction in order to experience a higher vibration. A Modern Priestess approaches her body, life and space as a sanctuary worthy of only what aligns with her evolved soul.

Chapter 10

Comparison

Principle: Compare yourself to no other.

*E*very person needs to validate, normalize and embrace the ups and downs of life on the journeys we each take. No life is the same. Comparing ourselves is unsupportive, but relying on one another for strength brings us the courage and power to continue. The Path of a Priestess is unique, different and very much aligned with transforming ourselves, our community and the world.

What most Priestesses do not realize is that we come *into our own* in our 40's and 50's. Wisdom is our ally and although we are old souls with innate wisdom, nothing can quite complete us unless we marinade and integrate our human wisdom with that ancient soul knowing. This takes time to come into harmony.

As women devoted to the Light/ Divine/ God, we are wired to be aware of others. We were created to serve others, and to pour love unto our brethren. However, in that service, we lose our way within ourselves, making it more about them, less about us and less about honoring that our differences make us all one.

When I compare myself to another person, I discredit my own journey (including my past and my upbringing). I uphold someone else's past and journey as more sacred than my own. I make myself smaller because I do not match someone else's greatness as my mind lies to me and tells me that his or her path is more valid than my own. I shrink, hide, pout and am unable to celebrate my wins (or the other person's, for that matter). My jealousy confines me to my darkness, obstructing me from feeling joy in the unfoldment of another Priestess and my own personal unfoldment. Her wins trigger my pain, and my own emotion envelopes all of my senses and actions. I become consumed with my broken self and separate further form the truth of unity and my own luminous Self .

But I also have moments when I don't compare myself to my fellow Priestess Sister. When I have healed my pain, I am open to acceptance and appreciation for who I am, what I have been through in life, and can appreciate another's journey. This is the inward journey of doing my personal work, of breathing first and then breathing life unto others. Personal power is born within me at these times, when the re-wiring of my brain, owning my shit, absolving others from influencing my reality, and most importantly, loving me first.

This self-love frees me from comparing my success or failure with someone else's because it frees myself from having to work on my weaknesses and focuses me on exalting my strengths. I am able to teach others to focus on what is good and right about themselves, freeing them from the habit of obsessing with what is wrong, or not to their liking because I have lived that aspect of being Woman. Freedom comes when I stop comparing and start being, and only being me—I invite you to try the same. It will free you, me and every other woman on this planet. Our own work creates a domino effect of opportunities for others to also free themselves from the oppressive hand of comparison.

This is the path of a Priestess: to focus on her spiritual and personal growth, without looking at everyone else, accessing where she is. As it turns out, a Priestess realizes there is no race, but that life is a long, seemingly never ending walk in the woods, where at a moment's notice, she will come face to face with God, and Light will pour unto her so that she may continue her walk uplifted. Coming in and out of shade, embracing light, every step of a Priestess is becoming more of who she was always meant to be in her highest expression.

Jealous Priestess

Being inspired by another is beautiful, but the moment when it causes inner angst, we must take the queue from our inner landscape and stop, notice our thoughts, acknowledge our feelings and be honest with ourselves about what it is that we truly desire. We cannot make our happiness and success based on our perception of someone else's accomplishments. We can, however, use them as a pause to access what our heart truly desires.

In order to be happy for others, we must first be happy with ourselves. Sometimes other people's lives can be the indicator of what we want. Most of us, at some point in our lives when asked what we want, have drawn a blank and think money is the only solution to all our desires. True, money does help, but we all know millionaires who have achieved this coveted goal and still feel unhappy because when the focus is only money rather than experiences, we lose the mark for what our heart truly desires.

Our heart cannot comprehend a pile of money, but our heart longs for warm air brushing our skin, the coolness and serene experience of the ocean water. Our heart understands little about granite countertops, but settles into cooking and hosting our dear friends all gathered in the liveliness of our kitchen. The heart wants experiences and each heart longs for different sensations, events, and how they are manifested. The wisdom of the mind knows the Modern Priestess cannot exist without funds, so the balance is truly to align both.

So, when you see a fellow Priestess finding the love of her life, be happy for her. If you have not been gifted this precious experience, know that what you thirst for is true love of your own; your Sister has been the messenger of this desire that wants your positive attention.

Imitation

Imitation is not the best form of flattery. No matter where you fall within the spectrum of this polarizing subject, there is great lessons in the words to come. You may feel triggered because this has happened to you, or perhaps you have inadvertently plagiarized someone's work or persona. You may be in denial and want to skip over this. No matter where you fall on this subject, read it because I assure you, you will be confronted on this at some point in your life. It may be with innocent things or it may be with an entire body of work. There is no judgement here, only opportunities for each of us to grow and align further to what is truth for our unique journey.

The logical next step to having clarity in your heart's desire is to look to the outside world to inform yourself of the possibilities. A social media post lures us as Priestesses to serve others in creating a soulful transformation, so we study someone else, modify their teachings and share them from the sincere desire to make other people's lives better. Yet we overlook something really important: although learning from others adds to our growth and our ability to share, we are creating further separation from our human-soul connection by taking their wisdom and calling it our own.

I have experienced both being the one modifying and being the one copied. What I had to come to terms with is that I was not fully integrated in my wisdom; I did not have my message, my teachings, and my process refined so I felt had to borrow in order to be effective. There is a way to borrow that honors all involved. Honoring one another in this Priestess Sisterhood is of the utmost importance. Having reverence for our Sisterhood is the beginning of a path of progress.

Reverence for a Priestess' intellectual property is not only the right thing to do; it is the lawful thing to do. We are not less wise to incorporate the tried and true knowledge from someone else. Besides, documenting our source is good science and provides further credibility to the longevity of our work. Basically, by crediting where credit is due, we let our audience know that we are legitimate, that we ourselves invest time, energy and monies on our own growth.

On the other hand, plagiarism reminds us that there are some people willing to speak in fake authenticity along with others who are not yet as secure in themselves. There are people who think that by taking another's words, posts or teachings that they are making it their own as a sustainable model. Sadly, they are mistaken.

Yet I have compassion for those who copy. As I look back at those moments when I copied, what I recognize is that I was not as confident in the Priestess of who I am. That is ok. I forgive myself for that. I also forgive those who do not see how amazing they are and think that copying someone else is good business. It is not. It is hurtful, void of integrity and causes more separation between the human-soul connection.

However, for the one who's intellectual property has been stolen there are many gifts. In some form, it is a test from the Universe to see if we are really ready to claim something we created. As my friend Michelle Vandepas noted, it forces us to ask ourselves if we truly want to be warriors for our own intellectual property. If the answer is no, then we walk away and fully let it go. Of course, if it tugs at you for years to come, at that point I recommend you re-think your answer! Having been writing this book for almost nine years, I know the tug, that back and forth. But I also know that as much as we are given chances in life, we must draw the line in the sand and decide where we stand.

Conversely, if your answer is a resounding yes, then the fun begins. This is the moment where you get to dig in your heels and commit. You expand your energy, extend your reach and fully indulge your desire to dominate this space as a Priestess of the Light.

The decision of *yes* requires fearlessness, not rhetoric. You need to strike your staff on the ground stating what and who you serve. Roar at those who dare to steal your precious gift. The Lioness within is not unspiritual, but she is a representation of the power you possess as a daughter of Light.

The Lioness pours love on this yes as well as on herself; she pours love on any one admiring her and pretending to be her. The invitation to heal receives love as it grows and expands on what has been provided, but she is clear to all that her territory is a sacred and no one can desecrate this sacred temple.

Clarity in the roar comes in many forms. With the intent of love for all, there is a way to be clear, concise and determined. Sometimes we have to seek the help of others, and sometimes the law can be enrolled to clarify the lines of what is appropriate and what is not. I am not advocating for blind litigation against those who steal intellectual property, but I am planting the seed for us all to move away from naiveté so that we appropriately protect our work. Although we all benefit from seeing everyone *in* the Light, we cannot expect everyone to be *of* the Light, and so it is important for a Priestess to have street smarts. Exercise discernment with those who have access to your energy and brilliance.

The combination of seeing the good in people and being discerning is not personal; it is about the sacred balance of value and humility. It is about each of us deciding that we say yes to our soul, our unique purpose and the goodness that we create when we share our gifts.

Free to be. You and me.

When a Modern Priestess embraces the beauty of her own journey and has a good understanding of who she is and what she is here to do, she not only let's another be, but she eases the grip on what she wants to achieve. A wave of trust comes over her as she realizes the prison of competing for a prize and begins to walk a path that aligns with her soul priorities.

Keeping score keeps her small and a slave to external measures, but walking through life on her own terms offers her freedom. Freedom in herself and for years to come, and freedom from the shackles of expectations she places on others. When a Modern Priestess learns to remove expectations from what she and others should be doing, she gains breathing space to be more of herself. At first this is unsettling and can leave her confused on where to go, but the more she spends on getting to know herself, the easier it will be for her to make choices that are authentic and sustainable.

Beyond her own terms, the Truth is that the Modern Priestess is the Beloved personified. She is the reflection of God herself on earth, and as such, comparing herself diminishes the pure radiance of her essence. A Priestess drops to her knees in the knowing that she is here to allow what is most holy to take over her life in the most exalting of ways. No sacrifice, but pure devotion of the Self reflected in her every word, action, and presence. The more she notices what is beauty within, the more the outside world reflects that back and comparison has no choice but to disappear.

Chapter 11

Sisterhood

Principle: Connect to a Sisterhood; it will Strengthen you.

$\mathcal{W}$ hen I have a moment of feeling how precious it is to be held by a net of women who see through my layers and into my heart, Sisterhood is restored. There are times when I can speak with my hurting heart on my sleeve and a silent Sister takes me into her arms, without fixing a thing but letting me know with the warmth of her skin and soft kiss on my forehead that everything will be alright, Sisterhood is healing. When each word I utter to a fellow Sister lifts her and brings her back to her most aligned path, Sisterhood is served.

The greatest gift of Sisterhood is when we know we belong and we are not judged. Being embraced for all our luminous radiance, for all of our obvious (and not so obvious) imperfections produces belongingness that is not just an emotional or spiritual esoteric experience, it is primal.

Thinking about who we have been as a species, it is clear that prior to modernity, our primal roots pull us into tribes to survive and rely on one another to exist as a unit. A lone wolf cannot exist in the wild as seamlessly as one protected by her pack. In the same token, a Priestess thrives in a Tribe. A Priestess moves away from survival and into safety, a sacred space as well as strength when she is held by legions of women who honor her.

A Priestess senses her connection to the whole when she is of service to her Sisters and experiences the cycle of giving and receiving. Biology does not lie. Based on a study at UCLA when women gather, stress levels plummet while oxytocin (love hormone) is released. We affect one another biochemically, emotionally and spiritually.

The Greatest Challenge

The greatest challenge to Sisterhood is the pain we cause one another. Nothing hurts more than the betrayal of words or actions by a dear Sister. There is nothing more offensive to our existence than knowing we wrongfully placed trust in someone who did not approve of or handle our tender vulnerability.

We hear of the brokenness of Sisterhood in work settings, where competition wins over collaboration. We observe this in the caricature and exaggeration present in reality TV. We have each experienced the vile betrayal by a Sister to a Sister, and yet perhaps knowingly (or unwittingly) we have done the same to another. Perhaps we are learning how to be in a Tribe, how to have reverence for our self-interest and balance it harmoniously with the good of all.

We are evolving in Sisterhood. We are learning how to incorporate being in Tribe and also exist in this modern world. A Modern Priestess opens her eyes to the truth of our current Sisterhood scenario; she understands it and addresses it with realness, compassion and a sense of tenacity along with commitment to heal the wounds of the relationships (and ultimately, the wounds within herself).

The primordial wounding in Sisterhood began with the reign of Patriarchy, and is mirrored in our relationships with our Mothers. The relationship between daughter-mother informs much of our experience of how to *be* in relationship, how to negotiate them, how to be in harmony with ourselves and others.

I am not suggesting that all our relationship issues stem from our mothers! Our mothers are the first experience we have of Sisterhood and in modern life, it is the primary one. In tribal settings, other female elders were readily available for relationships and would contribute to a more well-rounded (or at least greater variety of woman to woman) relationship. In modern times, we are left with the imprint of one relationship or lack thereof.

To place such pressure on one woman and to expect our Mother to meet and provide all our physical, emotional and spiritual needs seems in retrospect a mountain of a task. This is a woman who is typically alone in life, without a Tribe of her own to help her raise her young. Yet, we rely on this one relationship (for the most part) because it is what we know. The unmet needs play a record every day and to some extent, we look at some level to fill the gaps as we yearn to make ourselves whole.

There are spiritual reasons for this. Some of us come into this life with specific soul lessons and evolving tasks at hand; the parents we choose before we are born exist to serve this greater cause. Even the most painful of familial situations are there for a reason, sometimes beyond our comprehension. Most women who have overcome the layers of victimhood always see the fortune in their childhood because these experiences make them who they are. This does not mean to condone abuse or aggression in any way, but it is to provide perspective for the evolving Priestess. The healing begins when we forgive ourselves, our Mother, our lineage and our history.

The place of forgiveness does not lower the standards of the Priestess, but rather elevates her wisdom and perspective. It serves to raise her standard of what she is willing to receive in life, if she chooses to evolve. We can become complaisant as we accept the hand we have been dealt, or we can forgive, heal and command more. I understand that it is easy to feel defeated at times, wanting to give up. I recommend that the Modern Priestess choose the path of higher road, elevating her own vibration, therefore aligning with the choice to be whole. (And if she does not, I would encourage a lot of self-compassion, forgiveness and letting herself clarify how she really wants to be in the world.)

This does not mean ignoring abuse or becoming a mute to injustice. No! It means first heal, then speak and move mountains. Understand that sometimes in speaking, inner mountains are moved. There is no one way to evolve; the Priestess is encouraged to use her wisdom, her power, to practice assertiveness with compassion for all.

The Triggers

There is true power in being whole. It is always wise and always indicating to the Priestess who is devoted to growing what needs attention to be whole. Relationships provide the perfect petri dish if we take the opportunities and allow it. When a Sister triggers us, it is an indication that something within wants *attention to heal*. When I talked about *Live in the Now* and practicing *Presence*, these are the most graceful processes with the least amount of suffering. It is simple and requires practice. Owning our wounding, feeling it without over intellectualizing and stepping into the next moment second by second to feel what is alive, and letting this sensation ride through us as a wave.

If conversations are necessary, have them. But my recommendation would be to have them from a place of taking responsibility for our own healing, being honest with Self and practicing love for one another. We are all whole, yet we forget and mess up. This evolved form of Sisterhood allows each of us to have sacred space to be human, forgive, try again, love some more.

This is not intended to tolerate repetitive toxic behavior. If we find ourselves with a Sister who refuses to grow and take responsibility, the most loving and compassionate act is to say good-bye. Love yourself (and them) by walking away. Mourn the loss, let time heal wounds and clarify the desire of sacred Sisterhood by trusting that the seed we plant will grow to be a rooted tree, perhaps in another Sisterhood or Community.

The Most Important Thing

Modernity has taken us away from our tribal roots. But as biological beings, we cannot do life alone in a cave without bonding, without allowing another to deeply see all parts of who we are. Without the primal piece, our experience of life will be superficial. We cannot truly know who we are and how we fit into the puzzle of life without this honest, loving, integrated, sometimes messy experience of being in Tribe.

It is much easier to be a sage in a cave than it is to be in conscious and honest relationships where we are seen for all of who we are and where we are supported to hold this vision into action. I see Sisterhood not just as relationship with other women, but as a community that holds space for our best self to emerge. We are in an era where the Priestess is asked to bring the complexity of life and practice all the tools she learns in sacred community.

Sisterhood is the most ancient accessory and foundation to the Priestess, modern or not. As Priestesses, it is our birthright to experience the spiritual nakedness of Sisters. I will also offer that the next evolution of community, and that is that instead of looking for what triggers us, we shift our perspective and open our heart to noticing what is beautiful, holy, and precious about one another. It is important for every Priestess to take responsibility for her wholeness, but once she is fully empowered, the next phase is to see what is good and right in the world, and hence within herself.

Chapter 12

Permission

Principle: "Permission" is no longer needed. You are here to create with free will. Expand this awareness.

*I*t is easy to talk about courage and power, what is needed to free us in order to step fully into our power. Sometimes we may know exactly why we are apprehensive to come forward; other times, we are in the dark about stepping forward into the power, presence and influence to know of what we are capable.

Stories of other women inspire us. Movies bring us to tears as we see heroines overcome great obstacles while they fight for their right to be seen, to be heard and to live authentically. We may even have friends or mentors who have stepped through the inner transformation to breakthrough to honoring themselves and are thriving either with a joyous existence, financial success or both. But what happens when we know deep down that we are not intended to live a mediocre life? What is expected when we have gifts and wisdom to offer, though somehow we are not magnetizing effortless sales, relationships that honor us or experiencing overflowing support from the world?

When we know where we could be and see the mountains that separate us from this vision, we can tend to call them all excuses. Sure, we can internalize the shame, guilt and disappointment, but those thoughts and attitudes towards ourselves only perpetuate the sense of feeling small and inadequate.

What I have seen to be the most effective path is to stay in awareness of the thoughts, past experiences and conditioning that directs us away from being authentic. Awareness is first, and then it is systematically peeling off layer by layer, the masks we have been wearing for the world to accept us. Some people have the courage to do this overnight, and others, it takes time. Wherever you are, remember not to compare yourself. This is a Sisterhood; we are here to support one another, and to encourage each other to be seen.

Accept where you are. Love yourself no matter what, then step outside that comfort zone and stretch yourself to grow. Allow others to see who you are, the brilliance that you offer the world, and be bold even if it feels as though you are on a precipice without a net to catch you. Learn to expect that there is always a net. You are more resilient and strong than you give yourself credit. You know this. When you look back at all that you have been through, no matter how young or old you are, you know you are strong, you persevere. Even if you have had days or seasons where it hurt, you came back because as a Modern Priestess you care.

You care about being authentic, about making the world a better place. You know the time is ripe for you to leave the legacy of your gorgeous service. More than a Priestess, you are a Queen of your life and you are here to rule your

domain. Let's get started on this process of healing and acti-
vating your Inner Feminine Power and creating a life (career
or business) that is seeded from the power of your Queendom
for that positive impact you have dreamed of having your entire life.

Break Free

In the complicated world in which we live, the simplicity of who we are can have its challenges. Breaking free
from what our families, society and our loved ones expect
from us can be a process of deconstructing and reconstruct-
ing. The first decision to make is to no longer need to ask anyone for permission to *be, say, think* and *do* what our soul is
calling. Give yourself the green light to go—expect nobody to
understand, support or accommodate the new changes. Be
willing to decide, and then act fearlessly and boldly while taking one step at a time. Start small and then tackle the big con-
structs in your life.

In order to be bold, we have to be ok with risks.
These risks can rattle our sense of safety and are frequently
being misunderstood by those we love. We all have a need to
feel safe and understood. These needs are primal, and it is one
hundred percent normal that doing something outside the
routine of the Tribe is a decision that affects your primal
brain, which wants to maintain safety. The primal (survivalist)
brain's only requisite was to do everything possible to stay
alive; any individual threatening this is exactly that, a threat.
So, as a tribal unit, we are evolutionarily conditioned to stay as
one uniform group, doing what is known to be safe. The concept of individualism comes from a more sophisticated part of
our human development. Being more "evolved" threatens not
just our own primal system, but others who are intermittently
operating from this perspective. Take risks anyway. Stretch

your ability to move beyond safety and survival. Test the boundaries of how far you can go outside the tribal norm (whether tribe is family, colleagues, local community, online community or society in general). Remember that *we* make society, and the more of us that tap into the Rebellious Priestess archetype for our own happiness, the more we will move the needle closer to authenticity for all.

It is not always easy to break free. We only have to look at cultures that, due to war or other survival reasons, condemn any individualism. Take for instance Japan. It is seen as a more collectivistic society now when, as a country, it attempted to gain a stronger financial and global position. For a long time, individualism was not well received in Japanese business culture as a way to keep the common goal of collective progress as the focus. What I am proposing is not one over another, but both. I believe that if the individual is aligned to a Higher Power and connected to purpose, the legacy of her life contributes to the collective. We no longer have to choose between one and the other, but evolve both.

Conceptually, this sounds utopian. Practically speaking, it does not sound so difficult, but it would be irresponsible of me to propose this without reminding us of the obstacles and challenges this idea proposes. There will be push back encountered as we step out. Expect it and avoid the heartache of thinking all will be rosy. Perhaps I am wrong, and you will be met with full support; if so, then pat yourself on the back and high five yourself for being prepared without having to fight for being who you are. Positive expectation is an expansive choice, but preparing for appropriately based on our Tribe's ability to accept change is wise.

As we step into this bold path that defies what used to be normal for us and society, we will trigger others to take action, too. This triggering will seem like it is personal to us, but it is not. It is our inner fears being mirrored back, and possibly being expanded in this other person, who is secretly or without realizing wants to also access the same level of authenticity and power that we have claimed. We are each wired differently; some of us have an individualistic role to play and others a more tribal role to play. Connect to what is authentic to you in this dynamic and seek to align with the Light.

Activating the Feminine Voice

There is historical evidence that we have been suppressed as a gender. The voice of the feminine soul is not about words; it is about a deeply grounded wisdom that we harness in our core. I like to call it womb wisdom, which I discovered with motherhood.

The voice of the feminine focuses on taking care of her needs (yes), caring for her young (yes), but looks to the additional care and responsibilities such as being driven to feed all children as if they were her own. This is one of the strongest foundations of a world economy perspective.

The era of greed, profits at all costs, and oppression of those at the bottom of the *food chain* is beginning to crumble. The lack of the feminine voice in business is perpetuating an aggressive economy that does not value the health and well-being of the individuals. Further, this crumbling corporate perspective does not consider cross generational mentoring by employees, does not honor the unique and eclectic composition of the human population. The lack of the feminine voice in mainstream business fosters a selfish global perspective that alienates the value of giving, of helping others, of embracing community centric initiatives.

Companies may talk about work life balance and about maximizing the potential of the individuals, but few are concerned with how the feminine component of this community can contribute to more balance, to more job satisfaction, to increased employee retention, to creativity, to increased revenues and elevate the coveted innovation factor. These organizations ignore the fact that creativity and innovation typically happen from stillness (a quality of the feminine voice). Yet, few businesses are allowing this freedom and the expression of the feminine.

The voice of the feminine is not just about women. It is about the inner parts of who we are that understand the full cycle of life and the beauty of this cycle. To me the feminine voice supports each of us individually, but also the whole. A new reality of what is possible when we listen to the parts of ourselves that trust the gut feeling (the womb wisdom); the parts of ourselves that create partnerships that feel right in the heart and not just the head.

Each of us wants change. We want to shift. We want to better the institutions to which we contribute and ultimately we want to better our world. We realize that although we are evolving, there is more work to be done. The feminine perspective needs to bring this mindfulness and consciousness to business.

It is not up to corporations and institutions to change; it is up to us to bring the change we want to see in our place of business, and hence life.

Our girls are watching. Our young men are watching. They are observing how we handle life and business. They are forging the way for a new way, but make no mistake; they are very much influenced by what we are doing. It's time we, together, change how we approach and receive wisdom from the feminine voice in life and business.

We can talk about the studies that say that women in leadership outperform companies who do not have women leaders. We can talk about how results of the Credit Suisse Gender 3000 show the return on equity for companies with women in more than 10% of key positions was 27% better than for those with less than five percent and the dividend payouts had a 42% higher ratio.

But talking about that only feeds the old paradigm of constrained success. We need to start talking about *how* the profitability is important, but more importantly how positive influence and happiness are the real standards of success.

The feminine relies on the Priestess to move beyond intellect into the side of a thriving holistic experience, showing a path for all of those who feel stifled because they KNOW that life is more than money, approval, and fame. The activation of how acting on your personal truth can make a difference. An idea you have, can change the way a business does business, can change the way a product can create goodness, and the way lives are lived.

Competition is dead. Cooperation is about empowerment.

Power Discovered

Navigating this new found power can be invigorating for a woman. We notice this phenomenon when a woman gets a new job, gets divorced, or when she makes a life changing choice against the approval of society. She may find herself swinging the pendulum of her behavior and her perspective in life swing as far away from her normal. Some friends and family may express their concern of such new found freedom, and the focus of the Priestess is to not give much attention to it. The only way to land in authenticity of the Self is to explore the edges and truly exercise free will.

As long as a Modern Priestess is not hurting another human being, she deserves to have compassion for herself, to remember to not take others' reactions personally, and to continue to test the boundaries until she feels settled in her inner power.

This Principle asks us to look beyond society's norms, and with the alignment of the highest expression of ourselves, to safely experiment what we have deemed as taboo in the past. The activation of our power, our sexuality, and our voice in the world deserve to be expressed, even when society has tried to keep us in a box.

Chapter 13

Needs and Wants

Principle: Your needs and soul's wants are provided before you need or want them. Embody this intention.

 T he words in this Principle and Code embody the secret mysteries of building and multiplying wealth and abundance consciousness. Building your Queendom is your birthright; understanding the factors that determine whether this is your reality or not is essential to conquering this elusive formula for building wealth and experiencing true abundance.

Inviting us into the present moment, this Code reminds us that all is provided right here, right now. When we stay focused on what is before us, not conjuring the suffering of the past or the anxious projections of the future, we have a choice to acknowledge the riches in front of us in the *Now* and be grateful for all that we have.

This awareness shifts our reality because we start expecting the Universe and Life to always provide. It opens our gratitude for all that is available to us, allowing us to feel at ease and propelling us to understand that it is a co-creative process. It is not forcing things to happen or thinking that life is happening to us because we begin to see that it is an inter-dependent relationship. We materialize the spiritual while it works through us as it anchors the expression of the energy.

This Principle and the energetic shift we can receive from these words is a reminder that material wealth is good and right, and that we ought to expect that God has a cornu-copia of abundance awaiting our conscious awareness of such. The realities we may face compel us to think that only what we see, feel, and touch is real, but this Principle reminds that more lays ahead, when we believe to be true and when we practice the Intention to expect it.

Soul Development

The kingdom of heaven is available to every Priestess. Awakening the connection to the Divine is the true goal in life, whether we consciously admit it or not. Therein lays true wealth.

We are each at different levels of our spiritual evolu-tion. This is not about hierarchy; it is about moving through levels of learning. Similar to graduating from grade school to high school and then into University levels, the soul has a journey of depth and understanding. How deep our experi-ence is with our soul depends on how long we have been learning and how tenacious we are to stay committed to the spiritual path.

Some of us are Young Souls and some are Old Souls. Each one is here to evolve the soul through themes and as-pects. Some of us are here to learn about value, some humili-ty, some about love and some about compassion, but it's all different because each soul has a unique path. Many people try to offer blueprints to success, but the Priestess must walk her own road with eyes open, reaching for the tool, resource or person who can best support her growth and evolution.

This world can be a confusing experience for a Priestess. We are caught between two worlds and we decide our unique way in which we live the path of being a conduit between heaven and earth. Some Priestesses are learning how to balance their spirit work and their ability to create wealth, while others feel more comfortable within either the third dimensional realm (Earth) or feel more at home in the realms of the spirit world (Heaven).

For lifetimes, the two worlds have not always connected, but we are living in a time where a Priestess no longer has an Institution (or temple or church) to feed, clothe or house her. A modern Priestess is asked to establish a relationship that is void of co-dependence and based on being interdependent with the Universe as well as her own version of what is most Divine.

This is not necessarily about being an entrepreneur and gaining financial independence from an institution. It is more about an inner transformation, and an inner sense of resourcefulness and also establishing a harmonious exchange with her world. Whether a Priestess is employed, self-employed or non-employed is secondary; the most important factor is that she connects to the Source first and foremost and then determines how that inner alignment manifests itself on the outside. This means that a Priestess has direct access to the Source of abundance, and as she embodies this deep connection, she finds ways of expressing it. In turn, the symbiotic relationship creates a give-and-receive loop.

Authenticity

As I have shared, we have all taken on other people's expectations. When it comes to wealth, this is true as well. We live in a world where people value financial wealth. We try to learn from those who are most successful in the eyes of society as we try to emulate or replicate what they do, in order to experience the same level of power, freedom or lifestyle.

I am not saying it is bad to learn from those whom we respect and whose impact we position as a goal for ourselves. Quite the opposite: having models of what is possible are important for each of us, but we must learn to discern what will really work for us and what won't. We must be clear what is a desire we have superimposed from the world around us (or from our past of not having) and what is a desire that is born from our heart.

Outside wealth models can serve as barometers to us to try and test what is relevant to our inner happiness. In some sense, people we admire are examples that can inspire or trigger us into going inward to ask the questions…

Who am I?

What do I really want?

What do I deserve to shift inside me in order to receive what I genuinely and consciously desire?

Utilizing the wealth models in our society as indicators for what we internally desire and what we do not want can be a good starting point. We are all very clear that money has incredible clout on the impact we have on this world. Many Priestesses would serve the planet with their wealth in elevated ways, and the world needs women of higher consciousness to have more power in the world. So, those Priestesses who have a desire for wealth need to rise up and pursue such goals, especially those vested in contributing the goodness of the outcome of such wealth to the world.

We are not the typical example of wealth, nor should we use the current models of wealth as our markers of the power and impact we can make. Our job is to get to know who we are, peel the layers of the experiences we want to live, explore the feelings that we exude and create our reality (including our wealth) in our own unique way. Never forget that we are here to serve ourselves, but that giving back is a form of closing the loop of the give-and-receive abundance code.

Sustainability

How we build wealth has to be sustainable, meaning that we ought to be able to do activities that can work for us beyond short, get-rich-quick-schemes. If we pursue wealth for money's sake and ignore what is really right for our own happiness and wellbeing, we can find ourselves hitting burn-out because the goal of money for money's sake is empty. Our head may deny this, but the wise heart knows otherwise.

Being depleted from life, work and ventures that are out of alignment can take a toll on our psyche in addition to our physical bodies to the point of paralysis or even becoming sick. Most people cannot afford to be paralyzed for months or years, nor is it the way we are intended to experience our life force. In order to avoid the inevitable halt when we are off course, it is time we choose work that exalts our natural gifts, provides the edge for us to grow, and supplies us with the finances we want to feel safe and prosperous.

Needs vs Wants

If we are to see ourselves as emissaries of the Light, a different breed of human, we have to be honest of the differences between needs and wants. Only you can answer this honestly for yourself. Only you know what is truly a *need*, and contributes to being able to do the work you were put on this planet to do versus what is a *want*.

This is not to say that a want is a bad thing because a want is vital. Desire is vital to feeling alive. Long gone are the days when a spiritual woman denounced worldly possessions in order to claim the throne of spirituality and a connection to God. Yet understanding the difference makes a Priestess more evolved in her own inner world, and in turn a better decision maker. When we can separate these two, we can create our own success formula that balances whatever scale we choose using the two sides of our lives: need and want.

Acknowledging a need that seems trivial to most is also important for a Priestess to thrive. If a Priestess needs quiet one day a week and this seems like a luxury in the world in which we live, for the sake of authenticity and honoring her need, she must negotiate this in order to thrive and be ready to serve.

Poverty Consciousness

Feeling boxed by limitations of the mind or current situations can be an incarceration for the free-thinking Priestess. We Priestesses are intended to dance between the realms of Earth and the magic and mystery of the unseen world. We were created to enjoy being a channel between two worlds without belonging to one over another, but serving as the conduit between the beauty of the two. Forgetting our ability to thrive on this planet takes away from our power to be in command of our Queendom. It forgets our gifted connection to the Omnipresent Source and erases our unique dharma (our purpose).

When we feel disassociated from either world, we are making ourselves limited by only connecting to a portion of who we are. Priestesses can create both wealth and nirvana; it is our path. As Priestesses, we have access to envisioning the possibilities and beyond, and this is our birthright to exercise the privilege to be happy, wealthy and powerful. There is no need for guilt on days when we don't feel powerful. Before we go down the rabbit hole of darkness, we must find our way to stay connected to trust. Trust that all we need and want, from the perspective of the soul is our natural state. Faith in a Higher Power can guide us through the maze of life, keeping us connected to what we have come to learn, experience and contribute.

Trust

No matter how much affinity we each have for the material or the spiritual, things happen in life that rock our foundation, taking us off track. Most of us have limited understanding of why bad things happen to good people. We may have insights and also gather deeper understanding over time as to why unexpected things happen, but ultimately much of what happens in our world that seems void of goodness is a mystery.

It is challenging to explain to someone who does not believe in a Higher Power why tragedy is allowed to happen. Even those of us who have made it a lifestyle to *believe* are at times confused. We have a choice to either abandon the connection to the Divine or surrender to the perfection of a plan we cannot comprehend. Yet, the sadness or the anger that arises in each of us is one that can move us into action to bring positive change to the parts of the world we feel moved to contribute.

None of us can possibly understand the hurt of another, and my hope for each of us is that we find peace. Within this peace, we know that we are deeply loved; within this peace, we can rise above bitterness and plug back into the unlimited possibility this world has for us. Within this peace, we know we play an important role in adding more goodness to this planet. Beyond our human comprehension, there is a Divine and perfect plan to which we get to contribute for the good of all. One of the most fundamental principles this Code urges us to shift in our day to day is to see God as the Beloved; to trust that all that surrounds us is meeting a need and a want, and that if we should shift our perspective of what we expect, the nirvana we seek can be our reality.

Section Three:

Priestess Stories

Chapter 14

Why Stories?

*W*hen The Priestess Code was relayed to me, I had no reference as to how they would be implemented in my life. They generally felt like a good idea, but a bit out of touch with my modern lifestyle. However, I could feel that if I incorporated this different perspective of seeing and living life, I would be able to bring more balance into my life.

The Code demanded a more organic and holistic life rather than the rat race I was pursuing, and my mind struggled to comprehend how they fit with where I thought I wanted to go. Discovering that the only way to truly integrate them was to practice them, I began to notice how they affected other people's lives.

The interviews became an intimate observation. I noticed that some women were in synthesis of some Principles while others had fully integrated them within The Priestess Code. The women I interviewed simultaneously became my teachers and prompted me to discover aspects of this new way of living as well as doing business.

The way to ground any esoteric concept is to live it. The grittiness of life is the best playground to experiment and learn teachings from a higher perspective. It's how we move them away from our heads and into our body and soul. The Modern Priestess needs the grit of life to touch the hand of God.

This section of the book allows for you to access a deeper understanding of The Priestess Code, to learn from the personal stories shared and a gentle guidance on how to begin implementing this balanced way of living.

Chapter 15

Honoring Your Story

$\mathcal{S}$ imilar to a child desperately wanting and needing attention, our past can throw a temper tantrum. The stories of who we are, how we were hurt can cling to our leg refusing to allow the growth and re-birth we are so yearning to meet. The bonds of the over identification with this past is so strong that we begin to ask, "Who would I be without this?" Our ego stubbornly maintains the identity in an attempt to control and keep the soul from awakening our true state of being; blank divine canvases of creation with stories that flavor the way the painting may unfold.

We are left with our past as the only truth we know, and the questions of who we are or could be in this moment. It is as if all we know is the pain, and so it is all we continue to create.

Honoring Your Story?

Chapter 16

Framework

*B*alance: the seven-letter word most women utter in dismay at the task at hand. How to have it, how to be in it, and what exactly is it? Elusive, this balance can be. Most of us know when we are not in harmony with ourselves. It feels like stress, overwhelm, or void when we are out of Balance within. So, what stands in the pursuit of Balance? From my experience, it is partly the lies and stories we tell ourselves about what is true in ourselves and in our world, and yet the bottling up of the stories is what causes the resistance from such balance we seek.

We carry stories; stories from our ancestors, from our past, and from our current pain. Part of the space created by this book is to talk about the stories we don't want to discuss or have not been given a voice or audience to speak their truth for fear of being rejected or dismissed.

Many of us have a fear of tapping into a past that we prefer forget. This avoidance can possibly deter our complete healing. There is a balance in voicing the pain, opening past hurt, not feeling alone in the agony and all the while still have support as we access the unlimited possibilities when we claim victory over the suffering.

Most of us have not been heard. Most of us have not had somebody truly sit in sacred space and listen to what *is* real and alive for us or what defined us for a long time. In my experience something transforms inside when we have someone listen to our stories. And yet, if we met in a women's circle week after week and listened to the same story, it would get old, for those around us and ourselves. We know that when we focus only on pain, we only create pain. So, what is the balance here? Can we share our stories, feel relevant and alive, heal from the process of sharing and live a new life resembling who we want to be?

This section provides an opportunity to shed the stories by relating to the women interviewed for this project. It is vital that our collective stories be deeply heard, honored, revered, most importantly accepted, in order to bring the Feminine within all of us into healing and balance. It is time that we transmute this suffering because we have *graduated* from it as we are moving into a space of fully embracing all of who we are, not just the story of the past. We are here to create with free will instead of re-spun pain, to expand our awareness as expecting and living the notion that everything we need and want is provided in every minute.

In the book, *The Help*, by Kathryn Stockett, one of the African American women interviewed, shares the sense of freedom she feels after coming out with her story and truth. Although part of her may feel exposed, she moves into a sense of freedom; freedom that only happens when we are heard for the good, bad, ugly and most importantly, for the humanness and beauty of our experience. When we are seen, there is no more hiding; and that is the ultimate balance in being, from an authentic place deep within our psyche.

This book is a sacred chalice of sorts, holding our stories, giving them a place to transform into beauty, expansiveness and joy. Each woman decides to transform, but it is through being heard and acknowledged that she is supported, encouraged and strengthened to move through her personal transformation. Healing is a collective effort, and when we allow ourselves to be carried by a power greater than ourselves, the process can flow with ease and grace.

The stories presented support The Priestess Code Principles shared in this book; principles I received in a meditative state (or to be more precise in the blissful hot shower). Because The Priestess Code Principles are represented of the archetypal Sacred Mother energy, each word is supported by the channeling of healing energy. I am a messenger of the Divine Feminine in each of us (the Feminine aspect of God or Universal Energy), and as such, I bring you the message of the possibility and the reality of bringing our world into Sacred Balance.

We live in a world that has a strong Masculine influence; politics, educational system, corporations all have a very strong Masculine presence. The masculine in our world is out of balance, and the strength of the Feminine energies are ready to infiltrate our consciousness and world. The mind is overdeveloped (masculine), and it is time to soften and quiet it into balance, and it is imperative that we awaken our other bodies; physical, spiritual, emotional, sensual, ethereal, psychic, etc. It is time that we create space to invite and explore the realms of what it truly means to live in Balance.

Some of the stories may be hard to read. The pain experienced by some of the women is heartbreaking, but I have included them because we can each relate to elements within each story. What I have found is that the greatest discomfort awakens true spiritual growth if we have the right tools. If you find yourself uncomfortable, go back to Section One, "A Priestess Heals Herself" to help you feel the feelings.

Each of the stories relates to a certain Principle in The Priestess Code. For instance, when considering the Principle about Deconstruct, I have learned to not be afraid of the dark; literally and figuratively. I trust it a bit more, even if it is uncomfortable. I can now feel when a change is about to occur, and I have learned to let go a bit more. There are stories from those who are going through this phase.

Others illustrate the intensity of highest form, where I am reminded that God does not need me to accomplish anything other than focus on what my soul is most needing to continue to evolve. Of course my life is set up so that I work and I provide for my family, and so this Principle brings me more balance in remembering to only focus on raising my vibration, and that this is my only real job.

There are also the opportunities to see where we need to grow the most. The Principle of non-comparison and the lessons within it, remind me of the power of who I am because I am a child of what is most Divine, and the love I have access to because of my unique design. And, the most powerful lesson I have learned from connecting to Sisterhood is that I am not here to do life alone.

The more a Priestess knows herself, the more she lives from that place of confidence. Knowing ourselves gives us a curiosity of how our uniqueness can flow with life; we start making life more a dance versus a race.

Chapter 17

Listening

*B*efore The Priestess Code came to me, I had been exploring the seasonal aspects of each year. Although my mind was programmed to reach for more and more each year, if I paid close attention I could tell that some years were harder than others—some years seemed as though the stars would align with every project or venture, and others had me smack into a wall of resistance leaving me not understanding what I was doing wrong.

I began to move away from thinking there was something wrong with me or that I had done something wrong and more attuned to natural and organic patterns. There were years of *Yin* (quiet and inward) years and noticeably others were *Yang* (busy and active). Seeing myself as a *Seasonal Being* required that I accept each moment, each failure, each season in my life. I also had to unplug from my own expectations of success and to work with each season rather than against it. I began to explore how much nature has always helped me to clear my head, ground and remind me of what is truly important to me.

I have become an advocate of my own seasons una-pologetically, whether people understand it or not, regardless if they are triggered by me fighting for what I know my body needs. It has even become the way I communicate with my family about my seasons; I prepare them for either the Yin (and perhaps a little less income) or the Yang (having me be gone a bit more, and managing the influx if income). I have learned that I am a breathing ever-evolving Priestess and that my seasons need room to breathe so that I can feel connected.

When I asked Katie about her favorite principle, she wrote:

> *"The seasons will come and go in my life, but they will not come in the order I might expect. I do not follow the same schedule as nature. I am in winter now and hoping for spring and summer, but they may not come to me in that order. I understand that not all seasons come in order, and they do not last forever. Just as I can't stay in winter forever, I can't stay in summer either.*
> *"—Katie*

Radical Acceptance is the origin of a life of peace. Beyond accepting, it is allowing. When we allow what is to be, without judgement and resistance, life is free to flow and move to the next phase of growth or evolution. Knowing that all is in alignment with the Soul provides peace and perhaps even happiness.

We have learned as a species to nullify the raw aspects of who we are as Woman, and Man and Woman have forgotten how to accept, allow, love, respect the beauty of our wholeness. Most of us have been programmed to crave the lightness of life, and have not been given the tools to see the discomfort in life as a blessing. The *not easy* is a powerful ally to live and experience the full spectrum of the experience of life. We cannot be happy in summer, without, the inward journey and introspection in winter, nor can we get to the harvest without the use of compost to nurture the ground; one is not independent of the other, but rather they work together to complete a cycle.

We begin to see the beauty of the entire cycle, and focus less on fixating on final outcomes. We stop striving for the most socially acceptable season, but rather come to know the strength and beauty of each of the moments, and the enormous contribution they each bring to the whole of who we are. We use the time given to listen to what we are being told, so that we may come into our full and complete selves.

Many of us know when we are in dire need of rest, and for countless reasons we fight it. We do not set up our lives so that we can create time to go within, to embrace the winter within in order to keep our own self in balance. Part of the issue is our reluctance in taking the inward journey, and the other part is the incredible demands from family and society. We show up ready to conquer the world and yet we can barely handle one foot in front of the other.

We cannot always stop and be in the calmness that we crave. Because, let's face it, there are times when it is glaring before us that *I'm not just having a winter Monday, I am having three years of winter hell.* Yet, when we accept what is, the struggle crumbles and the Truth of the moment pervades. Sometimes the only action is to accept. So soft, so simple, and yet we need these words to be reminded. Accept what is.

And we do this in the stillness, the quiet moments as we listen to what the Universe and others are saying to us.

Moving Seasons

In the Northern Hemisphere the fall of the leaves is the queue to prepare for winter. As I sit in the healing circle and listen, I notice each woman's anticipation of the darker months ahead. Anna has moved to the city to escape the darkness of the country and will even go as far as fleeing to Mexico for a couple of months starting in January.

Somehow winter will follow her. Not so much the weather itself, but she shares a different kind of winter. The polarity between wealth and poverty is so stark when she travels south. Her experiences remind us that no matter how far we travel, the inquisitive deepening energy of going within is always present as its turn approaches. You can't out-travel winter.

Layers and Seasons

Louise felt the cold penetrate every layer of clothing and pierce her very bones. I looked to see her coat, and it was very flimsy, leaving her neck exposed, and it was a mere 60° F. She was struggling to warm herself with less-than-suitable attire. The beautiful part of it was that she acknowledged how little comfort she brings to what makes her uncomfortable. As she verbalized her hate of winter, she noticed that she was not really wearing a heavy coat and laughed at her own rebellion, recognizing that she has a choice to accept or not.

The discomfort of seasonal transitions invited her inner rebel to awaken. She brings us to this aspect of our internal and external struggle to accept what is, and to gift ourselves the gift of comfort when we most need it. Observing the journey of each woman throughout life allows us to see the ebb and flow of life, and an acceptance of the seasons of life.

Can we make peace with the winter within?

Tides and Seasons

Chandra's choice to marry comes from a feeling of being abandoned:

My name is Chandra. When I was born, they were expecting a boy. They had already picked a name for the boy. I felt I had to do so much to be worthy of somebody's love. It comes from abandonment issues; my mother was so busy raising three girls and I was feeling stuck in the middle.

When we believe that we are abandoned our defense mechanism becomes about protector of self, arising from fear. I would not take away any of the experiences I had; I am grateful I felt I was abandoned and blamed because if I didn't't go through that pain I would not have the depth to me, or be able to relate to people who go through that pain....it would be really boring!

I eloped at nineteen. He was Muslim and I was Hindu, and it was a big no-no, I was so attracted to him and I wanted to get married to him and I did. I was looking to escape from home. There were so many rules and I was such a free bird, this felt like an answer. There were signs very loud and clear not to do it. The next day he took me to his family, who did not accept me. I created that torture and that is what made me real.

I can't say I have all the answers, but I have to live it! He took me to his family, and they treated me like an outsider because of my religion. The irony is inside I was separated from my divinity and outside all I got was separation. How can I embrace anyone when I could not accept my own divinity?

(She recognized her painful, but powerful and wonderful journey of accepting not just her seasons, but her entire journey, which continued when she met a married man and had an affair, then left her husband to rebuild her life with her children.)

I am not a divorced woman; I am a divine being. I am not a single mother; I am a divine being. A total reminder to myself with such a deep and embedded pattern that it keeps coming back. And now I am so aware, and I can breathe into the discomfort and not have to bring a story to make it ok. I can just experience my breath and invite more divinity into me. At a soul level I knew it was my path to help others, even when I was broken.

Anger Reveals Truth

Erica tells us how anger for her is a different entry point to creating:

With anger, it's like I put my foot down and say enough. It's a contrast to what I want; anger helps me get super clear. Anger can give me juice to create. It's an emotion and has such raw, potential energy.

I used to think the fire part of me was not ok. Finally I've come to know it is me. I was given that because I was brought to bring social change. If I'm not pissed off enough, I won't change. Most of us tend to make changes from crisis or chaos. It's how the majority of people do it. It gives me energy to change things. I know suffering is saying I'm sick enough of this, and then I am willing to do anything to make it different. Human beings are feelings and emotions.

Setting intentions is great, but feeling and passion are the wind beneath the magic carpet that makes it move. Intentions are not enough. The emotion makes it alive.

I always try to have this attitude that I am being shown where to expand. I get excited when I see where I can grow more because it can give me more happiness, joy and vitality. It's like being a treasure hunter. It makes it fun, light and not so serious. I get excited when I find a treasure. I get to come away feeling whole.

Desire to Live

Toward the end of my interview with Licia, she said *The inner me says 'Fuck you' a lot...* Here's why:

I decided a long time ago that I was not going to perpetuate the secretive crap of sexual abuse. A lot of people don't want to hear about it. Even people who have not had the experience don't want to hear about it because it makes them feel so uncomfortable. And, of course, there are people who don't want to hear about it because they have experienced it and have not done their healing work with it. Because then it's "in your face" and there is something uncomfortable that is brought to the surface and they don't want to hear about it.

So, I finally said 'Fuck it.' When I talk to people and they are not cool with it, tough shit you need to deal with it. This is real. It is happening to people, a lot. And it is my life and my life experience and therefore I am not going to hide it.

She felt her throat clearing up, and she pointed to this being a symbol of her third, fourth and fifth chakra closing up. So she set the intention that cleared her throat completely, and she said, "I choose to talk about this freely, easily, with grace, and integrity."

And shared her story of sexual abuse, of observing her father being abusive towards her mother, who was sexually abused when she was a little girl. She had a lack of allies, a mother who hated her as though she was her worst enemy.

Years later Licia's life now is utterly blessed. She owns her past and speaks her truth.

Peace and freeing herself from her past to relish in the joy of healing. She has learned how to show the way through the barrier to overcome hesitation and fear, to drill in to that wall to get to the bliss. Her childhood prepared her to be an outspoken woman, and there is a perfection and symmetry in being heard by the collective because if we are silent, if we don't share our perspective and life wisdom, we are withholding the answers to the questions that the world needs to hear.

Gentle Voices

Orion said little, but her few words communicated her angst:

I have internalized the rules. I don't even know if they are my rules - subscribing to a linear way of thinking that is faster and more logical - your labor is a product of time or output.

I feel that I have gotten far away from my values and understanding my voice. I've gotten away from my own voice; I have gotten far away from me because of money, financial value, and my job.

But you know, I have to work and I love it. I love people. I love the collaborative office problem solving; it is intellectualizing and energizing. What appeals to me is service, figuring out something for someone. Helping someone be who they are capable of being. And also the colleagues: constantly figuring out what I should be doing and what's the answer. The collaboration and the service are fun... but it lacks boundaries for me... I have lost what is sacred to me.

My breath gets me out of my head into my heart, and then I can ask, 'How do I feel in my heart?'

Honesty

An extremely well-educated woman, married to an Ivy League scholar, Carrie illuminates the struggles of a woman accepting who she is, step by step. She shares of her deep depression and her toned down rage. She asks point blank, 'Why do we have to put a front?'

She chose to explain to her then two year old, *Mommies get sad*. Carrie's husband is very supportive, but she is uncomfortable with *his* decision to have *her* home school. She admits, "If it was me, by myself, *I would not even consider it.*"

Her Priestess gets buried; she second-guesses her own self:

I'm willing to give. I trust him; he's so passionate about home schooling. I don't have an opinion about it. I don't have that kind of energy or passion. I know it would be fine either way.

But is it? Sometimes it all starts with questioning.

Grace

Seven years prior, Gloria was faced with her fears and her pain. Being a stay-at-home mom, running a home-based business with her husband and being haunted by a desire to study Nursing, she felt completely paralyzed with her fear of math and science. She decided to take a mission trip with her church and was a translator in Honduras to the group traveling. She soon found herself following and translating for the medical team and became immersed and enamored with their work, their compassion, and the people they were serving, and making one of the most life changing experiences:

I had what you would call a Godly, mystical experience, there's been several, but it was interesting how life brings you these life altering experiences. This trip... I had this feeling of I'm home, I'm back home. And I'm here and why am I here? Feeling lost. And one night, I was up and I could not stop crying, weeping.

All of a sudden I stopped crying and heard this voice that said, 'You can do something', and there was silence, and the voice said, 'you can go back to school. Conquer this fear and anxiety that you have of these classes, and become a nurse, like you were called to do.'

So I felt such clarity, I had no fear. We are really all wounded individuals. We are hurting; if we are honest and can talk about it. And I think most people are not willing to go to the depth of the soul and heart, and that is when the healing comes. When you can go deep. And go to the hurt of the pain.

What a gift. I have been able to find healing in healing others. When I tap into my own pain as I hear the stories of others, I am healed. It's such a beautiful thing to experience.

Create Space to Release the Past

Stacey was in her second year at an Ivy-League University in Massachusetts. Coming from a small town in the South, she was used to being a big fish in a small pond. This big-eyed, aspiring fish quickly became a small fish in the ocean of cut-throat competition. She found herself competing for everything and constantly being pushed and shoved by peers all looking to get ahead.

Not knowing where she belonged, she questioned her worth. She quickly constructed strategies to escape. Sex became one of the ways she gave her power to her peers. She said her promiscuity led her to situations that got out of her control, including date rape. As she struggled to stay afloat, her subconscious went to work.

Stacey feels that she manifested her ovarian cancer to have a good reason to leave this harsh, competitive, judgmental and unsupportive space in her life. Coming from where she came from, she could not justify to her family and herself leaving a path of such promise; she would then be coming home a *failure*. So, cancer she said, *was the easy way out*.

She recovered from it beautifully. After ten years of thriving after cancer, Stacey held on to her *dirty little secret*, as she called it, until she met her healing muse.

This new relationship has forced her to face things that if she were alone, she would choose to not deal with. But she doesn't want to hide anymore. He was challenging her because she was challenging herself. She verbalized pain to him, shared the deep pain about cancer and that's when she let the past go and was released from being trapped in the story:

It is not about him loving me, but about me choosing to stay present as me in my relationships.

Lemons Into Lemonade

After twenty-one years of dedicating herself to one job and one company, Kaely's anxiously seeking her next step. As an environmentalist trying to convince developers for over twenty years to build with environmentally conscious methods, she is tired. She is tired of trying to manipulate them by finding economically favorable reasons why they should care about wetlands. She says most people respond favorably once they understand the impact projects have on wildlife, and yet she also knows that some people just don't care.

She is tired of her own colleagues too, whereas she would like to be enthusiastic:

I want to look back and say, I was doing good, rather than I was being good at my job.

When I read her The Priestess Code Principle "You are here to be the Highest Form of who you are and nothing else. Love that." she resonated with it, re-worded it to fit herself more: *I want to be a good person; what is good for the earth is very important to me.*

The conversation quickly moved to her marriage. Kaely has been on an incredible roller coaster marriage ride:

At work I don't have support and respect; I don't feel I'm the person in charge. The reverse is true [at home]. I'm the mover and shaker. In some ways I resent that because I wanted a better support system.

She realized that she had choices and she had help, and was free while fully naked in her authenticity.

Know Thyself

Nancy's wisdom of decades supporting entrepreneurs is fully aligned with this Principle:

I have daily practices that I have for years and years, where I get up earlier and I meditate. I write in my journal, do some visioning; I pray. Just things that I am doing that help me to keep me grounded and then I go and I do my day.

In my business, I always talk to people about what I do in my business. But I don't always talk about in depth about my daily practices and how if it wasn't for that, I wouldn't have the ideas I get from my business. I wouldn't have the intuition I use to able to help my clients. These days, I am actually taking the time to talk to people about it in more detail, to emphasize its importance and to incorporate it into the work I do with my clients. It is a part of it now and what came to me was I need to have more ceremony and less seminar because I work with people.

Spiritual practice puts you more in touch with your intuition and when you have your intuition activated, and then you can hear your inner voice. When you can hear your inner voice, then you have better decision making abilities and you can understand what to say yes to, what to say no to. You can also get clearer on what you're doing and why you are doing it. So there is a certain focus that comes into place. I see this huge ripple effect of benefits when you understand yourself. Then when somebody comes along and says, 'ok, I want to super impose my model over you, you have to wear this outfit,' you can say yes or no from a place of real truth or real knowing.

It doesn't mean that the person who sells the most or has the most successful business is the most intuitive or grounded. It is something that you can feel inside of yourself, it's self-satisfaction. I really think that other people pick up on it, too. They'll say, 'There is something different about you, you seem more real, more relaxed. I feel more connected to you; there is something that feels really different here.'

The Body Speaks

Mirna came to know the wisdom of the body at a very physical level. She came to my house excited to be uniting with a group of women we only knew over the phone. In this world of technology, enlightenment (or at the very least knowledge) is accessible via the phone or a computer. We had both taken classes from our mentor and this was our time to meet her in person. Not just that, we were to meet some of our fellow virtual classmates. So exciting. Yet, the moment came and disappointment and judgment set it. She began to compare herself to the other women; to their success and to their priorities.

Mirna's body reacted with intense abdominal pain as she continued to sit at the dinner table. She could no longer sit in the presence of her judgment and excused herself. We quickly left dinner. Her classmate's priorities were not her own, and at this moment she was struggling to accept that her two young boys were her masterpieces. She had boxed herself into a certain Divine mission and she forced this upon herself, her family and the world. And the world did not respond with open arms. Her business was not flowing, she was not inspired to shift that, and she was scared to admit that.

Weeks later, one of the greatest gifts Mirna received was *permission* from a friend who told her, *You can create a new life purpose.* She said that such an invitation was eye-opening and allowed her to see that she is the master of her Divine co-creation.

The Triggers and Healing of Comparing

Michelle, the beautiful *Miss Venezuela*, model, TV and Radio Personality is my childhood friend. She had bought the *Miss Venezuela* dream; the dream that by becoming the coveted role, she would receive her ticket to happiness, fame, and greatness.

When I talked to her she said, *"Desde que era pequeña, no unico que queria, era ser famosa.* (Since I was little, the only thing I wanted was to be famous); *hoy dia soy famosa, y siento un vacio* (today, I am famous, and I feel empty)."

After years of chasing and catching the fame she always wanted, she feels like she doesn't know herself. An abrupt cancellation of her show caused her to escape the scrupulous public eye, who *comentan todo* (they comment on everything). She decided to do more radio programs for some time.

This provided her the opportunity to spend more time doing what she loves. After at least ten years of being in the entertainment industry bubble, as she calls it, she is giving herself permission to *be* Michelle.

This would not have happened had she not seen the perfection of having a door closed so that another could open.

Fashion Photography

Shannon is a high end fashion and boudoir photographer. She has dedicated her work to shinning a light on the theatrics of fashion, and helping women as well as young girls see themselves as beautiful as they themselves see fashion models. Many place blame of the insecurities women face on the standards the fashion industry projects. Shannon's perspective is both enlightening and empowering to some.

She doesn't think the fashion industry is to blame for all of people's problems because people are projecting onto the industry their own baggage. It feels easier, more convenient to point the finger at an amoebic monster than it would be to have to address the pain we feel with ourselves.

Part of Shannon's work is to show people a part of themselves they rarely acknowledge even exists:

This is less about theatre and more about using the elements of fashion and theatre to bring out the side we hide; the side that is real. Sometimes it is confidence and power, and sometimes it is pain and the power that comes from letting ourselves be witnessed in it.

People take photos of themselves to post on social media, being deliberate with the images they let others see... But the second someone else pulls a camera on them they freak-out and freeze because they don't have control over what's being produced. They don't see what someone else is seeing; I think the reason people freeze up is the lack of control. People are not comfortable or used to being vulnerable with themselves.

But no one admits to vulnerability.

Religion

Wendy was the most popular kid in our four-room school. Boys ran with her as she leaped past them and excited both their competitive nature and their interest in girls. Girls wanted to be her or at least close to her. She was funny, smart, athletic, and pretty. Before high school, her family moved back to the United States.

I was left with nobody I liked, trusted, or enjoyed quite as much. I was left to find a new group of friends. This was not the last time such void was present in my life. Prior to my commitment to work on Sisterhood, this was my pattern. I would get close to someone; they would leave. Every time, I would have to mourn the loss and trust that someone else would come along so that I could share what I most cherished, and that I could be the same for them.

As I struggled to find community time after time, I asked myself if I could actually expect - and find - a circle who would laugh, shop, meditate, tell me when I'm so off base, who are there for me at all times, with all judgment aside, and who yes, indeed inspire me and I them? And let's be honest... can I be *that* idyllic friend right back?

I grew up going to American missionary schools. Although I have resented past Christian friends for not bringing me into their most intimate inner circle due to differing views of God, the purpose of a Sisterhood, capital S, is to support the spiritual growth of the individual and the collective group. In order to support such growth, the members have to be able to fully get behind the intent of the individual. So, a Christian friend who only sees redemption or spiritual success through a relationship with Jesus Christ, who does not deem any other interpretation of the Divine, may have a hard time fully sharing with a Buddhist. (I am not suggesting that all Christians are this way, only providing one potential example where the environment is one where people feel safe and respected).

I do not think a successful Sisterhood necessarily means that all members must believe the same thing. On the contrary, the friction in the differences can allow a Modern Priestess to explore the edges of her comfort zone, as long as mutual reverence is a pillar in such a community.

On Facebook a Christian acquaintance, Krista, posted a question asking people if they saw a difference between friendship and fellowship, as described in the Bible. She wrote:

> *I was asking about "fellowship" from a Christian perspective. It comes from Acts 2:42 "They devoted themselves to the apostles' teaching and to fellowship, to the breaking of bread and to prayer." At least for Christians, I think we're called to do more*

than spend time together, but that "fellow-ship" should include friendship, but also en-couragement, purpose, challenge, "spurring one another on towards good deeds"... etc. Not sure what Webster says though ;)

...I do agree that as women we do need to be connected to one another. Women who can-not be friends with other women (and there are many of them) are missing something... something important. And there's something wrong there; it's not natural. We were made to be in relationship with one another. In our church, we have LIFE groups that are meant to be small communities of people coming together to study the scripture, pray for one another, and to have fellowship & accountability with one another. We're trying to "do life" together - to let one another in. We have some co-ed LIFE groups, but far and away, the best groups are the ones where we're separated. My all-women's group is where I can speak freely; I am comfortable enough to really be myself. We can share our ideas and thoughts about life, relationships, God, and all sorts of things. We have trust and love for one another. It's my sisterhood :)

All Shapes and Sizes

The journey of a young single mother, Channel shares what or who supported her:

And there it was, the moment of truth. The secret that my body had kept to itself had now revealed itself on a little stick. How could this be true? And me, Channel, out of all people. My mind raced and my heart dropped. My world had just been forever changed within a matter of those three minutes. I was eighteen years old and still a senior in high school. This was the time I was supposed to be preparing for prom and parties, graduation and college acceptances. And here I was, sitting in the corner of this bathroom crying my eyes out and biting on a pillow to keep myself from wailing. I was going to be a mother. I had to come to terms with it. I kept it a secret for a while, no one besides my daughter's father and I knew. But as we all know, some secrets will reveal themselves on their own. And so did mine.

Telling my mother was the hardest of them all. I had failed as a daughter. I had failed as a student, sister and role model. But God works in mysterious ways and on a cold night in mid-January in a church, I, with the help of a preacher, told my mother that I was expecting.

I had lost a good amount of my friends; the more weight I put on, the less I even wanted to step out of the house. I even had family members putting me down or aside.

Within the next few months I received a phone call that would change my mindset of life and how I would view myself as a mother. I remember the first call from a healthy families home visitor, she explained the program and told me how I was referred to her... My home visitor became my supporter. When people including my own family doubted or fostered negative thoughts in me, she would be the one to turn it around and foster positive images of what I could do for myself and by myself.

My home visitor helped me focused on my goals and told me that although I was a young mother a baby wouldn't stop me from leading the life I wanted to and succeeding in the goals I had for myself prior to becoming a mother. My home visitor also instilled the bonding between caring for myself and my child. It took a while, but within time I no longer cared what people said or thought about me. I wasn't going to become another teen statistic. I graduated high school on time with a diploma. I then went onto a junior college where I studied part time to earn my associates degree. I am now a full-time student at a state college where I am studying to earn my bachelor's degree in communications.

I've made it a personal goal of mine to foster positive images of parenting and child and parent bonding whenever I can. I'm happy to say that after being a healthy family's participant for almost four years, I am now working for healthy families as a home visitor and hope to motivate and inspire others as inspiration and motivation had been inspired in me.

Success is not measured by what one brings, but rather by what one leaves. And I hope to leave a profound impact on the hearts of those who I touch and their children for years to come.

Impermanence and Infinite

The path of motherhood makes Erin question her place:

I don't have a social circle. There's the mom's community, but most of the activities are during the day. I want a community of moms that I can talk to… but I have no time. We have a two-year mark that we are shooting for… I'd love to be part time; I would love it with her and myself.

Asking time for rest and to relax into who we are is a lost tradition. So many of us live lives of service to our families, work, and society, but when it comes time to ask for rest and relaxation, we are stumped. I often have thoughts of requesting time for myself. When it goes to the time to ask, I don't do it. It feels frivolous and I feel guilty.

It is less about me and more about all of us as mothers. We have moved away from a tribe, and I keep moving to different areas that support me, but we don't have the social support. My husband needs a brotherhood, too. I need to find, seek, and create a sisterhood, so that it allows space to find clarity.

Friendships, Trust, History

My new friend, Stacey, offered to help me with a project and we began talking about putting things in order. She shared:

I am at the point where I know there are different levels of friendships, and I take things less personally. It's not like in 7th grade where friends become part of your identity. I have different friends for different reasons. I do have one best friend; I can talk to her about everything. She's older; I call her My Wise Old Owl Friend! She's very knowledgeable, calm, and can pull her life book out and say she's been there and done that.

Those who I have known the longest, who are forgiving of my flaws, get to see all of me; those who know me and know where I come from do, too. Who have seen me not achieve my dreams. Who have seen me get divorced. There's history. All that history can make for a really great friendship. That's who sees me.

It is a choice. It takes work to get together, to continue to know each other. You accept changes as you go through them. There is a connection throughout time; you are more accepting with what is going on in life. It's a choice to engage in the small talk of life or sit down with a cup of coffee and share who you really are.

Yes, my wisdom is built on fear. Fear of being let down. Disillusioned by people. Fear of being hurt again. Over time, you get to know them. If they are transparent, which is rare. You get older, you say how much do I give, do I need to give, and am I willing to give?

I've learned to protect myself. I've had people use personal information against me. I've gotten burned. We all have! You are taking a risk, and sometimes you do hold back a little. And you do take a risk with every new friend you make. Just take it for what it is right now.

Homework

Pam's earlier path has given her a key to insight:

When I went away to college, the way I dealt with a lot of my home instability (such as my mother begin volatile, physically abusive, and even destructive) was to work, to put the old things behind me. I was a really sensitive person, really intuitive, a healer who really didn't know she was a healer, growing up in a home where no one knew about that, it really wasn't allowed. That was the strategy that I learned was to be invisible and just really not create any trouble as one of six children. All money from high school jobs went into an account. I worked full-time in the summers. Any gift I ever got, the money went into my college account.

When I came home from college for sophomore vacation, my dad told me to get out of the house. I left, and I didn't know where else to go. One of the girls that were on my floor in college, where I was an RA in my school, lived about a half hour away and she invited me to some family function. Her parents heard about what was going on with me and they invited me to stay with them, thank goodness. I ended up staying with them.

I went home within a week or two, to empty out my bank account, but it was already gone. They stole from me. I sat down to talk to my mom, she told me, "Well you didn't pay me for gas, electricity, or food or clothing so you owed me."

I really felt I was that girl trying to be perfect. You know, trying to do everything they wanted me to do so nothing would go wrong, and it still did.

So, I went back to New York and kind of fell apart. I failed a class. I started drinking heavily. I was accused of a robbery. My boyfriend broke up with me. It was one of those times, where you hear people talking about like having that, Phoenix-ashes-rising; you know everything was going wrong. I felt like I was getting pummeled.

I wound up lying my way into an apartment, because at that point school was over. I had no place to go and I had no money. I told the real estate agent that I had a job that I didn't have. I was just trying to live day by day like something was going to work out. And the real estate agent told me - without me saying I needed work, 'you know, there is a chiropractor down the street that is looking for someone to come and work for him.'

Somehow I got that job. I have no idea how I got that job. Later, the chiropractor said this psychic had come to him and told him I was coming and he should hire me. He did hire me and I started working there. I didn't really like it, the culture of it. I thought the people were kind of wacky. But, I was trying to stabilize a little bit.

Yet here were these strangers worried about me. My boss told me that I needed to drive to be adjusted by this guy. I did it because I needed my job.

He said to me, 'your body, your nervous system, perceives that it was under attack at an early age and it just got locked there. Whether it was under attack or not I don't know, but it perceived it and never got out of that state. And so what we want to do is adjust your nervous system to allow it to unwind that so that you can remember more of your pure and natural way of being.'

So he adjusted me; he did this light touching. I had this really simple vision moment of seeing curtains blowing in the wind, like, like the window was open just a little bit.

It was just so simple, I don't even know what that was, I didn't even really think about it. I had decided I was going to chiropractic school. I had never thought about being a chiropractor, even though I had worked in my chiropractor's office; never, ever considered it. I just decided I was going to do it, and someone told me I should go to a university in Atlanta, and so I just went.

Even that's a part of that is not asking 'permission'. I just did it. I knew I wanted to do what I felt would heal people. I knew from that moment I felt on the table. Just that moment of relief, of more light, of more space, and more air in people like me who didn't have that.

It was very hard for me to learn because I had to feel. I had to feel myself; I had to learn to feel other people. I had to feel a lot of pain, and unwind all of that pain. I would touch people for years and I wouldn't feel anything.

But one day I felt. It just kicked in and all my training, and all the information, and all the experience I'd had. I could feel things and know what was happening on a deeper level and I can just tell more. But it took a long time for me. And I started to feel a little bit more comfortable. My patients were guiding me basically to learn what they needed to learn.

One of the concepts in chiropractic that there's a unique intelligence inside every human being. I mean it isn't just defined in chiropractic, but it's in other holistic traditions. We are born with this unique sense of who we are. There is this unique intelligence of this inside you of who you are. Two cells come together; you divide fifty times and create a hundred trillion cells that are communicating with one another. Rapid speeds, doing multiple tasks of syncing with other people, so that's how women have cycles. Somehow all these cells innately know how to do that and to sync to the planet moving, and it's pretty dynamic with this intelligence that's inside of us.

That inborn intelligence is something that is a guiding principle for me in my life. And, even in raising my children. I think that when it comes to women and their roles, sometimes I think about the roles for me, like what does it mean to be a woman? What does it mean to be a daughter? A mother? A wife? A sister?

Instead of me just being this innate human, I'm serving the role sometimes. I personally, don't really love that. I don't love serving the role because I feel like it is a meal that society that is serving on a dirty platter that I don't necessarily want to take. I really try to think innately, 'What is it that I desire to give myself, my children, my husband, my mother, my sister?'

I wasn't finished, but I'm still not finished, and I don't think I ever will be.

Token Male

I set out to interview women, and women only. Perhaps the cliché of including a gay man is a little obvious and for some a little obnoxious. I no longer see people as one thing or another, I notice energy. The energy I notice about my friend Michael is that of embodying what we perceive as Feminine principles in the most exquisite of ways.

Similarly to most women, Michael had to persevere, fight a little, hope a lot, and has finally manifested a life where he is accepted for who he is:

I guess it was probably my teens. It had something to do with the dawning of my self-realizing my sexual identity, my sexual orientation. And it felt like the only way that a man would love me, which is what I wanted, was if I was a woman. And you know, I came to realize that was not the truth. And even in the gay world, even in the gay community, I am feminine. I am totally not alone in that. You know, I would say that I'm in the top ten percentile of femininity, at least in being comfortable with that.

I've always had these qualities and I think I sort of cut myself off from them because it wasn't really accepted. I mean, to some degree I was lucky as a child. I could do macramé at home; I could get away with being creative in my house, even if it I sort of pushed the line as my mother was more tolerant and my dad less comfortable, much like our society was. My grandmother championed my creativity and we would go to Michael's Crafts and decide together what 'Mikey' was going to make.

Even with the higher level of acceptance for the feminine in my house, I still denied some of those aspects and I'm just now at fifty years old embracing them; thinking of myself as a healer or intuitive, or any of those sort of feminine embodied qualities. I've never let myself really take that in fully. I am in a place to allow myself to feel that. I think a lot of that has to do with self-love and self-acceptance.

I'm in a place of joy and acceptance in spite of all of it. That has to do with my awakening spirituality. And, I guess desire to thrive and a desire to be part of the solution in some way. That is kind of who I am as a healer and I allow the universe to participate instead of always trying to do it alone, which I had done most of my life.

It jogs your memory of the path you're supposed to be following and I feel like that's happening for a lot of people. Maybe it doesn't always start with self-love, as in loving myself. But I do not want to hide who I am not feeling bad if somebody doesn't like me. Being able to say what I think. It's not big stuff, but it's basic stuff that I have denied myself. I'm walking around and feeling good. And it's expecting good things to happen and not somebody seeing who I really am and having the house fall on me.

I listen to spiritual people talk about what it all means and how we can stop it from getting worse and I want to help be a part of the solution. I hope I can be part of the solution, part of that message and making sure my kids are getting that message from me as a parent.

What I am clear about is that I need to take care of myself. And if I'm always taking care of other people, then that can't happen.

Hitting a Wall

Shea reflected about her birthing process:

I knew I would devote myself to be a mom, and I knew it would at some level change my life. And that was scary to me to lose my freedom. I really love to be able to come and go and now that was going to be interrupted.

I was really, really, really responsive to pregnancy hormones, once the hormones kicked in, I wanted to stay pregnant forever. Somehow becoming a parent has been very humbling and I don't have much judgment regarding choices women make anymore.

In the middle of labor, I hit a wall. I didn't want to be a parent yet. This part of me was refusing, like a little girl in me who wanted to be free and mobile at her will and be able to have no complication, and I was enjoying pregnancy. I was in real grief about giving up that feeling. I had never been happier. When the surges came, the crashing surges, my body was complying w/ my resistance. That ring of fire was freaking me out. Miraculously, my body slowed down. I didn't want to do it yet.

I was thinking, 'Would someone please save me?' because I didn't want to push that baby out. I had all these expectations of what would feel good. In my mind I was failing to take advantage of the strong contractions; all these judgments happened. I was mad at everyone. Nothing was working. I tried to rest; I was getting intense contractions and shakes.

Then this knowing came over me of what I needed to do. I heaved-hoed. Then the angelic hands of the midwives arrived and she came out. It was an amazing moment, of shear knowing and simplicity and of it being very earthly and organic.

When I think of all my processing, sometimes it is just about being in the exact moment.

Defining Value

Susan believes *When the Children's needs are tended to, THEN the world will change.*

Actual needs are very different than programmed needs. She says clean water is a basic need, and these basic needs also become commercial exploitation:

Water that is clear, clean, unpolluted. How do I create fresh water for myself? If I meet a need for myself, then I must be asking for the whole community.

It's similar to sanctuary. That's a safe place to sleep, a place to center. When I meet that need for myself, it has global effect. If I know how to create sanctuary for myself; then I know how to create it for other people. This is sufficiency as well, teaching others to fish for their sanctuary.

The key is to understand, recognize needs and who you are at your core. 'Who am I and what is my value?'

If you don't know, then you feel that you have no value. This happens when you determine your value on what you could contribute in the work place. When I started opening, it helped me work on my intuitive side, the energy in my own value to offer the world. And that started happening.

I now have pride in my work. When I struggled financially, there were 900 agencies funded by taxpayers' money that were ready and willing to be of support. If there is not a need, those agencies would not exist. Yes, there are people who take advantage, but I think it's a minority. There is corruption, and that does exist.

I am saying that there is help out there. I moved into self-love and self-care; what I asked for, I received. When I reached that lowest point, I found my authentic place. And when I got to that place, I felt more love for myself more than I have ever felt for myself.

Balance in Yourself

Amy shares a perspective many of us can relate to:

I'm very smart and cautious about it all, but I know that there is still something that is not ok about doubting myself and my skills and what I have to offer. Given the skill sets that I have, given the success I have had, I should be making comfortably a lot more money. I should be able to ask for that. In fact, I am in this process of doing just that... It is terribly deep and deeply embedded.

If I could remove one feeling from my energy field, it would be the feeling of lack, that fear that there is not going to be enough money. It's uncomfortable when I look at my situation. I've managed to save money so that I can take a medical leave of absence and take a trip. I've been smart about it, so it is not really lacking. I don't have to feel that it is lacking anymore. That fear that there is not going to be enough is what I am trying to deconstruct.

It's hard to hear people talk about leaving their jobs because it hits me on a very primal level, right where I get that fear. I've worked hard to not have that response. It can still creep up a little bit. I think getting rid of the fear that I will not have what I need will be helped by determining how I can replace the fear. For instance, I can replace it with the belief that my work is so valuable, and I know this at such a deep level.

The difference will be that I am going to literally stop apologizing. I am not going to go out of my way to accommodate and help someone who does not see my value. I know that I need to create more balance; I belong in the picture. The difference is going to be that I don't have this bizarre guilt of working more hours or working harder.

Humanity is in this great place of transition where people are looking for something else that works. I know that I have a different model, and I know that what I do is incredibly valuable. Somewhere deep in me I believe that what I do is valuable and people will pay for it. This is not just about the money, I have to do this, this is what I have to offer it to the world.

A Life of Privilege

Jess offers insight about another side of privilege:

I didn't consider myself privileged growing up until we moved. My grandfather was a huge person in a small town; the social and monetary privilege or power my grandfather represented was in my life. The kids were cruel, mean, making me feel isolated and alone. They resented my last name. Their parents forced them to invite me to their birthday parties, and they let me know it.

I had difficulty having social acceptance. It's hard on kids to have no friends. When my family moved to Toronto, Canada, I could retreat without everyone knowing my last name or assigning expectations. This time I had trouble being accepted as because I was an American and it was assumed that I felt superior, but I didn't feel that way.

Privilege is a dirty word. Some people revel in it, and I don't. I've had to learn to accept and live with it. I don't shun it. I could use it more in my jobs, but I want to be known on my own merit. I want what other people want.

I would hope that I give respect. I didn't get respect as a kid, so I don't care where you come from, I treat you with respect. I want to give back as much as I can. With privilege comes responsibility; a lot of responsibility... I can't change who I am.

My desires are like everyone's desires. My purpose is to give back.

Chapter 18

Bringing it Together

*N*ow that we know the Principles and have received the activation of the words in the Principles, the practical piece comes when we frame them in our day to day life. My suggestion would be to take one Principle at a time and re-read that section, observe it in your life, journal on it, notice where you could use more focus or help. Inspire courage within yourself to step outside your comfort zone in order to embody it more.

These Principles make sense to most people, but our mind doubts the validity of them. They defy the paradigm of our world. When we allow them, they really infiltrate our psyche so that we bring more of the balance they encode. Although they seem different, there is a central theme to them all: accept who you are, connect to nature, grow and expand when necessary, express who you are, you are a precious child of God, and trust all will be provided.

In many ways, if we like the way we feel by reading a specific Principle, we are forever changed if we practice it in life. This may be scary for some people because it can mean that they have to leave behind everything they had deemed as precious and worth pursuing in life. But as I have studied these Principles, I can tell you that they are gentle; they work with our timing and what we can handle. They are organic and natural. They are here to make life more full.

If they were a person, they would want us to ease up on the pressure we put on ourselves. They would not want us to fall asleep to life, but rather to open our eyes to the preciousness of what surrounds us, even when it does not feel pretty. They remind us that there is perfection in the plan that is beyond our human comprehension. Life does not have to be hard.

In fact, life is not supposed to be hard. It is supposed to be full of grace, even in the ups and downs. Have gratitude for every inch of who you are. Love and support one another to anchor more harmony and balance. Speak of victory. Hope for what you most want in life.

Serve well and live through the motto: *Feel Good, Be Wealthy and Give Back.*

When we have all three in harmony, we receive the essence of what we need and want in abundance. The beauty of these three as markers for whether our lives are fulfilling is that each of these mottos is strong without being bound by traditional net worth. Whenever we doubt if we are truly walking the path *The Priestess Code* awakens within us, this motto serves as a compass and guiding light. When we enter a new season, we can remind ourselves *I feel good, anchor my wealth,* and remember to *give back.*

Feel Good

One of the gifts Millennial Priestesses offer us is that they value feeling good, and with that they bring a wave of giving important to a life of pleasure, self-care and freedom.

Self-care and wellness have revolutionized the Modern Priestess. Before, we accepted burn-out as the norm. As mothers, we are demanding *me time* and families are complying and understanding how important it is to fill our own emotional and mental cup first to serve.

As women (and men!), we are tired of *going* and we are beginning to crave a pause. Beyond that pause, we all value creative lives, careers, and relationships that *Feel Good*.

We are raising our standards for what we allow to exist in our lives. This, my Modern Priestess is a good thing. Of course we all have to do things we do not love sometimes; that's at times a part of life. But we are certainly not tolerating 80% of doing what we hate anymore. We are actively planting seeds that feed the fruits of fulfillment and harmony.

Our only job is to keep this *Feel Good* mantra alive in our yearly intentions, quarterly goals and weekly to-dos. Discovering what feels good to us is our compass to actually enjoying this life experience and making choices that lead to a life void of anxiety and filled with connection.

Be Wealthy

Most Priestesses could exist in the land of *Feel Good* if we were given a choice, but the truth is that many of us have come to feed children, run non-profits, be entrepreneurs, run corporations and basically guide the planet.

We have responsibilities sometimes beyond ourselves and we are conscious enough that we do not run from them. As Sheryl Sandberg says, we *Lean In*. Besides, we also know that *Prosperity is our Birthright* (from Prosperity Manifesto by Karen Curry Parker). We have come to cash in on this monumental time in our planet where we get to exercise our power to grow our influence and command our Queendom.

As awakened Priestesses in sacred commerce, we also recognize that wealth is beyond the material, but we do not hide behind spiritual speak or poverty mindset. Being wealthy means negotiating pay for our value that meets our needs and wants. Also, as we mentioned, it is our responsibility to do the inner work to heal the resistance, belief, pattern or feeling getting in the way of receiving compensation for our skill and wisdom.

When a Priestess does exchange her day to day for financial pay, she receives the love and reverence that honors her effort. The wealth we create does not define our value, but it is a beautiful vehicle to heal the parts of us that feel small as well as denote the outer representation of what we offer.

Time and time in my work with clients, I have seen doubling rates or negotiating raises to be one of the most powerful work I do. It is an important that a modern woman feel her power.

I would caution us all to re-read the previous sentence and become aware of what happens (the triggers that have risen). Remember that I am not saying this is a one size fits all, and I am not saying that if a woman does not earn money she cannot access her power. She may feel very powerful being centered in poverty and that could be her journey, but if that is not the path you desire then I invite you to explore your Money-Power-Worthiness relationship.

I have seen the Money-Power-Worthiness balance play an instrumental role in hundreds of women healing aspects of old hurts, that sometimes go beyond the woman herself; it can be lineage and it can be collective pain we get to heal by accepting that we are now free to be powerful, if we choose.

As a gender, we have been oppressed, put down, and kept small. Slowly through policies, waves of feminism and spiritual connection, we are coming out of dark days and into times when it is ok to own property, get equal (or even more!) pay, and prosper in life and commerce. This is all relatively new for us in the past three thousand years.

This is an incredible breakthrough for our species and can affect men in a very profound way as well. Historically, men have been bound to taking care of the family. Although role reversals or changes are not always easy to adapt, I think it is for the better to have balance, if that is what is right for the individuals, relationships and families. It is important to remember that one role does not define us. In such transient modern times, the roles of a woman can change dramatically from her journey of being single, married, having children/ no children, to entering her later years. One answer is not right for an entire life; sometimes it is right for one to five years. It is ok for us to be flexible with our Truth.

When a woman knows that she can provide for herself and her loved ones, then she can be in a partnership that is void of co-dependency, even if the situation is that she is being provided for 100% financially. Having the belief that she is capable of sufficiency releases her from any bondage; she becomes free to give and receive without feeling unsettled in her financial stability.

As Wealthy Priestesses, we have to be smart about receiving financial value, budgeting, saving, investing and being generous, and let's remember that being wealthy is spiritual too.

Give Back

Up until October of 2015 I had been leading and coaching women on how to *Feel Good + Be Wealthy*. Even though my husband and I have supported key non-profits through our work, I had not incorporated it into my curriculum.

But during a Soul + Business Retreat that I led, something powerful came over me and I launched with tears and quivering lips a monologue on how my heart ached for children of the world, and yet how I saw them as sacred and whole. I see children as whole and I see every one of us who has a roof over our heads and food everyday as advocates for them. Wellbeing and wealth cannot be the only objectives of a Modern Priestess. I could feel that every woman in that cozy, loving space of the retreat agreed and felt herself moved to always include *Give Back* as part of their life and business goals.

We all get so wrapped up in our own needs that we can easily forget the people who we do not get to see on a daily (or yearly) basis who need our help. We keep poverty at bay for fear of being infected, but really it is compassion of which we are most afraid—if we were to feel their pain, we'd know exactly what to do: give.

Each Priestess is in her own soul journey. Some are here to learn wealth stewardship, some are here to detach from money, some are here to practice giving fully, some are here to balance both giving and receiving. Again, no one answer applies to us all.

I would recommend spiritual mentorship around the triggering topic around giving and receiving and anything pertaining to Abundance. It is best to gain perspective on where we are and where we want to go to grow spiritually and as human beings. Awakening the sacred relationship of giving and receiving is our birthright.

The Priestess Code is a path of balance, a path of awakening to the beauty of what surrounds us, and the beauty of who we each are. The Code is a reminder of deconstructing from insular lifestyles, and instilling the importance of community. Each Principle speaks a truth that is sometimes dormant inside us, and that is longing to come out and play, even when others do not understand. The Code is about our journey of exercising our Feminine Power and with this bringing harmony to a world that longs for it.

Bringing it Together

About the Author

*R*epresenting a compilation of over twenty years of study, practice, and testing, The Priestess Code is not *in line* with my training as a Molecular Biologist! Leading up to this mystical experience, I had been working in the biotechnology industry for a large Fortune 500 company, doing Sales and Business Development. I was making a great income, traveling, working from home, carrying a leadership role and my confidence hit a pinnacle when I gave talks at Harvard University, Yale, Brown, etc. Part of me felt accomplished, proud and in awe of how far I had come from growing up middle class in a developing country.

The other part of me felt disconnected to my family, sad that I had to fly across country to sit in boring meetings, frustrated that my colleagues would waste time when I had precious children, and ultimately I felt dead inside. I could see parts of me dying as day after day I became I slave to the salary, the luxuries it provided and the sense of feeling stuck and confused by the life ahead of me. I hit a wall, a breakthrough or meltdown really. I could not take it anymore, and I prayed, pleaded, made deals with whatever was hovering over the ceiling of my home office. I asked to be given a way out.

A week after my *breakthrough*, the Universe gifted me with a lay-off accompanied by six months of severance and a beautiful commission check. I sent an email to everyone in my personal life and invited them to participate in a beta test for a class I was about to start running; *Reclaiming Your Power*. Of course, this class was more about me reclaiming my own divine power, but as they say, *we teach what we most need to learn*.

I started with twenty people on the phone as a group; each of us seeking the authentic power we knew was inside, somewhere. Through the participants in this class, I fell in love with being a woman. I fell deeply in love with our collective experience of being Woman and also my heart touched the deepest empathy for our collective pain. I heard the pain, and I wanted to alleviate it, yet parts of me wanted to bypass my own pain. I wanted to tell their stories, to alleviate their most hidden thorns. Almost every woman I interviewed cried during or after our interview.

It was not enough that I be curious about them or for them to open those wounds and the blessings from the lessons learned; I had to communicate my intent and reverence for their journey. Some women came to my home, some sat with me at their kitchen table, some met me at coffee shops and others talked over the phone. I listened, asked questions and allowed them to recreate their most delicate secret. It was very intense. It affected my functioning as a mother and wife. I was at times disturbed, haunted, and radically affected by the stories. The way I processed and integrated these women into my psyche, took me to emotional places I had not known within myself. Today I realized that I synthesized their stories from a limited paradigm. I had become a vessel for them to transmute their pain and thought that liberation could *only* happened in this way. I was wrong. The darkness swallowed me. I had to put the manuscript aside for years, and revisit when I felt strong enough. Then something shifted, I began to see their stories not as painful recounts, but as holy expressions of the Sacred Feminine. Instead of searching for pain to heal, I began to crave what is beautiful in life.

I have learned from great teachers in my life. I am in the practice of having Balance. Some days I am fully awake and others I miss the mark (though the Principles remind me that there really is no *mark*, only this present moment where we are invited to live our path, and only our path and always notice the beauty and the access we have to whatever it is we desire).

These Principles and The Codes are for the Priestess who is ready to soar in life and who wants to *Feel Good, Be Wealthy* and who feels the tug in her heart to *Give Back*—these are the essential messages within The Code. The teachings shared here are for those who are done feeling blocked or stuck; women who want to get to know themselves deeply, intimately, in ways that perhaps no invitation has ever presented. They give the mind a place to rest, and invite those who are ready to come into life fully present. When we experience The Code, we learn that part of ourselves we knew existed, but have been afraid or too lost to uncover.

In doing so, the world outside becomes luscious, colorful and abundant. These Principles are unique to each and every one of us. We get to define them. There is no dogma. It is about beginning a relationship to them as a guide to building a relationship with the Divine Feminine within ourselves. We each get to decide what each Principle means.

Let's allow ourselves to become part of the collective Sisterhood of women who inhabit this planet. As we indulge in the surrogate healing, we discover that we really are one with these women, and if not our own pain and desires depicted, our mother's, daughter's, sister's, friend's stories sing throughout these pages. In some ways they have paved the wave for us to begin anew and to see that the Beloved is our friend, confidant, and ready to assist us in the unfoldment of our highest expression.

Ironically aside from my coaching and start-up advising, I continue to work in the medical industry. My life is at a place where I make all of who I am work for me. I have not mastered each Principle, but they have become my path to being a Priestess in commerce and service. The process of embracing all of our facets is a dance and an opportunity to truly know who we are. Sometimes this happens as an ocean wave and sometimes a drop at a time. This journey invites Sacred Balance. May you find the sweetness in life through awakening the part of you that yearns to be fully present and alive.

To learn more about Asha's retreats, coaching, start-up advising and speaking, please visit:

http://www.ashaisnow.com

CPSIA information can be obtained
at www.ICGtesting.com
Printed in the USA
LVHW040441100320
649438LV00004B/115